it's
REALLY
10
months

D1456645

it's REALLY 10 months

Delivering the truth about the glow of pregnancy and other blatant lies

Natalie Guenther, Kim Schenkelberg, Celeste Snodgrass

Omaha, Nebraska

© 2014 Natalie L. Guenther, Kimberlea M. Schenkelberg, and Celeste M. Snodgrass

The information in this book is true to the best of the authors' knowledge and their ability to relate it. While the authors have endeavored to present the content accurately and honestly, the authors disclaim any responsibility or liability for errors, omissions, or the accuracy or reliability of the information presented. By using the information herein, you assume all risks associated with the use thereof. The authors shall not in any event be liable for any direct, indirect, punitive, special, incidental, or consequential damages, including and without limitation, lost revenues or lost profits arising out of or in any way connected with the use of this material.

This book identifies product names and services known to be trademarks, registered trademarks, or service marks of their respective holders. They are used throughout this book in an editorial fashion only. In addition, terms suspected of being trademarks, registered trademarks, or service marks have been appropriately capitalized, although the authors cannot attest to the accuracy of this information. Use of a term in this book should not be regarded as affecting the validity of any trademark, registered trademark, or service mark.

The phrase "It's Really 10 Months" and the stork image are pending Trademarks of Anam Cara and their respective owners.

Paperback ISBN: 978-0-9888668-1-2
Mobi ISBN: 978-0-9888668-2-9
LCCN: 2013934172
Library of Congress Cataloging information on file with publisher.

Design and production: Concierge Marketing, Inc.
Printed in the United States of America.

10 9 8 7 6 5 4 3

Celeste:
To Anna and Bobby—this book has always been only for you.

Kim:
To Ben—I was the luckiest person on the planet the day you showed up on my front door. To Mitch and Trey who make being a stepmom easy! And finally, to Giselle, Aslyn and Gavin for one amazing adventure!

Natalie:
To my husband Brad, my one and only homerun. Also, to our amazing boys, Gage, Jace and Tate—looks like we knocked it out of the park.

ACKNOWLEDGMENTS

We wish to thank the following people:

Dr. Robert Bonebrake—thank you for your willingness to meet us for lunch and be so easily coerced into providing your expertise and fantastic sense of humor. We are eternally grateful. May each patient that walks through your door be as lovely and well balanced as the three of us.

Cecile Oliver—your vast medical knowledge helped us deliver the truth.

Our editor, Sandra Wendel—thanks for thinking we were funny, believing in the book, and letting us keep WTF.

Lisa Pelto and the wonderful team at Concierge Marketing—you helped this dream become a reality! Thanks for your willingness to work with three crazy, opinionated, hilarious ladies who could only meet on Sundays.

Tracy O'Donnell—thank you for capturing the essence of Anam Cara with your creativity.

Mary Ann Gomel—thanks for catching our good side and photoshopping the other.

Laura Peet Erkes—thanks for being the best 4th wheel.

Thanks to the mom bloggers who paved the way and established a sense of community.

NATALIE: Brad, to have you as my biggest fan means more to me than you will ever know. My parents for always believing in me no matter what crazy idea I came up with. To my sister, without your support and free babysitting this book wouldn't be here. For my extended family and amazing friends—you are my soft place to land. To my partners, Kim and Celeste— iron sharpens iron—I am a better human because of you both. Anam Cara!

KIM: I want to thank my husband for his constant support of late night and weekend meetings. You are the most competent and capable dad I know to manage all five kids and their activities without the blink of an eye. I love that you are such an engaged and attentive father. I want to thank my parents for their encouragement in all my endeavors but especially this book. You know what I mean. Our kids are beyond lucky to have you as their grandparents! To my friends and family I would like to say that your never ending support helped to keep me inspired during slow times and all the times between. To Natalie and Celeste, the connection we have through our experiences and this journey are embedded in my soul. I cherish the many moments of laughter to the point of gasping breath and tears.

CELESTE: I would like to thank: John for loving me even when I haven't had a banana. Your love and support mean the world to me. Mom for believing in me and believing this was a book when it was just thousands of funny and rambling emails and for never giving up on this dream. O'Mama for instilling a love of reading and (hopefully) good grammar.

O'Papa for paving the way in the publishing world and giving me someone to live up to. Jennifer for reversing the roles and becoming my wind. Natalie and Kim – with you, so many things have taken on a new meaning including crop circles and eye of the tiger … but the new meaning of friendship is what I hold most dear.

From: Your Editor
To: Natalie, Kim, and Celeste

Seriously? You used 1,487 exclamation marks! As your editor, I just want you to know that in editing the mountains of emails among the three of you, I preserved your words but eliminated the excessive exclamation marks, dashes, periods, and question marks. I toned down some of the swear words (not all) to make sure your readers didn't have to close their eyes *and* ears. Otherwise, these are your exchanges during your pregnancies, and readers will just have to understand that you (and only you three) are responsible for the content, tone, and outrageousness of these actual emails. My work here is finished.

Contents

- One more joyous side effect of pregnancy: carpal tunnel.
- Words to live by: When in doubt, listen to The Beatles.
- Muddy dogs, repairmen, and meltdowns—oh my!
- What is your definition of granny panties?
- The Va-J-J, wild and unruly.

- Stretch mark cream on the feet.
- Does anyone else experience midnight puking?
- It's okay to be leaking from parts that don't usually leak, right?
- Do you think the massage therapist will rub my butt?
- Does the waistband of your underwear touch your bra?
- I thought this massage table had boob holes!
- If this is labor, I don't like it.
- What's up with this snot in my shorts?
- I kicked my doctor in the nuts.
- Heidi Klum is a skinny bitch.
- My lips are swollen—no, not those lips.
- I'm having a c-section so I don't poop during labor.
- Yes, girls, I peed my pants.
- I will be pregnant forever.
- Squat and bear down.
- This can't be it. I didn't shave my legs!

- How much stool softener is too much?
- Crying in the shower is the latest trend.
- Who said breastfeeding is the most natural thing?
- How did we get from ice cream to sex in three seconds?

Introduction

To: You
From: Celeste, Kim & Natalie
Subject: You have GOT to read this

No one ever tells you about all of the crap that happens to you when you're pregnant. For example, it's not nine months it's ten *long* months. This is just one little lesson we learned along the way.

This book is for anyone who wants to have fun, who wants to laugh, who wants to know what it is like to be afraid for your baby, who doesn't mind poking fun at herself, who can lay it *all* out there. Even if you never have any intention of being pregnant, you can laugh with us—or at us.

We are three thirty-something women who were fortunate enough to be pregnant at the same time. We began sharing our questions, fears, humor, and experiences through emails, which became a lifeline and virtual support group. We are here to tell you the good, the bad, and the ugly of our experiences. We do not hold back for the squeamish or the faint of heart.

We are all social workers with graduate education and met each other while in college. We all worked on the obstetrical unit of a hospital for several years. Celeste and Natalie even worked at the same hospital. But working in the obstetrical unit is *nothing* like being pregnant yourself!

We started writing these emails in April. At that time, Celeste was due in October. She is married to John and is the official "go-to" gal for pregnancy information since she is already the mom of two-year-old Anna. Because Anna wanted to enter the world butt first, she was delivered via scheduled c-section.

Kim (due in September) is pregnant for the first time, but she has already had a taste of young ones through stepparenting her husband, Ben's, two boys (ages five and ten).

Natalie (due in August) and Brad are the total rookies in the group.

Along the way, we thought it might be helpful to have someone sane weigh in on our hormonal ramblings. We unanimously agreed that Dr. Bob, a specialist in high-risk pregnancies, would be our most likely ~~victim~~ candidate.

This is just our story. It is not in any way guidance for anyone. We really did listen to our doctors, though, and we *tried* to follow their advice. If you are pregnant, you need to listen to your doctor also.

So prop up your cankles, rest this book upon your shelf of a belly, and check our email log. You deserve it. You've earned, or are about to earn, your badge of honor known as motherhood—however the hell you got here. We made it through the entire experience and lived to tell the tale. And you will too.

Meet Dr. Bob

Our medical expert is Dr. Bob, known professionally as Robert G. Bonebrake, MD, FACOG. He is a partner with Perinatal Associates at The Methodist Perinatal Center at Nebraska Methodist Women's Hospital in Omaha, Nebraska.

He is also a Clinical Associate Professor in the Department of Obstetrics and Gynecology at Creighton University School of Medicine as well as Clinical Associate Professor in the Department of Obstetrics and Gynecology at the University of Nebraska Medical Center.

Dr. Bob received his Bachelor of Science Degree in Mathematics from Creighton University and his medical degree from the same university. He served as an intern and resident in the Department of Obstetrics and Gynecology at Creighton University and then completed a fellowship in Maternal-Fetal Medicine at the University of California, Irvine.

He holds a Certificate of Special Competence in Maternal-Fetal Medicine from the American Board of Obstetrics and Gynecology. He is a Fellow of the American College of Obstetricians and Gynecologists and also of the Society of Maternal-Fetal Medicine. Dr. Bob has special expertise in perinatal ultrasound screening. He spent more than the first decade of his career in academics serving as a Maternal-Fetal Medicine division director and director of perinatal services.

He has numerous publications and has given many formal presentations, with special emphasis on antenatal diagnosis, complications of pregnancies, and the management of pregnancies at risk for early delivery.

But the real expert on pregnancy in his family is Dr. Bob's wife who is the mother of their six children. He relies on her for advice from time to time. One of the many qualities that endears us to Dr. Bob is his open acknowledgment that despite his numerous qualifications, his wife clearly knows more on the pregnancy subject than he ever will.

April

From: Celeste
To: Natalie, Kim
Date: April 23

I am sooo flippin' tired—but my real complaint is about this weekly email I get that tells me where I am in my pregnancy and what the baby looks like and how big the baby is and what not ... it about made me want to puke today. It says that my baby is about 3 1/2 inches long and about the length of a lemon—and that it is enough to make some women have a little pooch ... and I have a big fat pooch and feel like a cow. I want to hit the person who writes that email.

I really don't know anything else—but one of my friends is coming to town on Thursday, and I need to figure out how to tell her about the pregnancy on Thursday night at dinner. Any grand ideas on how I should do that?

From: Natalie
To: Celeste, Kim
Sent: April 24

I understand! The part with the jelly belly was hard for me. Still, sometimes when I lie on my back and push on my stomach

I can't feel the baby ... so obviously there is some room in there that is not filled with the baby. It's a terrible process. My belly is huge. It looks like a soccer ball. And to my horror after I eat, sometimes my boobs rest on my stomach ... WTF? Skin that used to lie flat on my stomach now is horizontal. It's not good.

I couldn't think of a good way to tell my friends either, so we all went out for breakfast, and I said something like, "I'm pregnant. Pass the cinnamon rolls," and they just stopped and stared at me ... it was pretty funny.

Delivering the Truth

Body image during (and after!) pregnancy can be tough. In the first stage of pregnancy, you start growing out of your regular clothes but don't fit into maternity clothes—so then you just have to buy larger clothes and feel fat. ☹

 From: Kim
To: Natalie, Celeste
Sent: April 24

Did you get pictures from your initial ultrasound? I wonder if you can scan them and print them out and do something fun with that? I know I recorded the baby's heartbeat the first time we heard it and emailed it out to everyone to see if they could guess what it was ... That is about all I have in the creativity arena today.

From: Celeste
To: Natalie, Kim
Sent: April 24

I really enjoyed your boobs resting on your belly story! Unfortunately (or fortunately depending on how you look at it) I never experienced that since my boobs are even tiny during pregnancy. The largest I ever got to was a large B cup. Pretty sad.

On another note, we have decided to sell our house and look for a bigger one. Pregnancy is good for me. When I was pregnant with Anna, I got a new car. Now with this one, I get a new house. ☺ We talked with a real estate agent and the house is going on the market this weekend! Talk about fast!

May

From: Kim
To: Natalie, Celeste
Sent: May 1

Boobs: if you really don't want to hear about them, then I suggest you delete this message before you go any further.

I went to Victoria's Secret yesterday to get measured for a bra since my current bras are leaving purple indentations everywhere. Now, I would like to insert my disclaimer here that I had tried going to Target to buy an el cheapo bra and I even tried on nursing bras. None of them fit.

So off to my old faithful Victoria's Secret. The girl measured me, and I about fell to the floor! I went from a 36B to what we thought was a 36D. When I tried on the 36D, it was kind of poking out a little on the sides so I actually showed her what was happening (normally no one sees me try on bras).

She said, "Oh, it looks like you are a little too big for that bra."

What! Where do you go from a D? Meanwhile, two little punk-asses were standing outside the dressing room waiting for their "ladies" as my very helpful gal went to get a DD. (Again, I almost fainted—isn't that what size Pam Anderson wears for God's sake!)

She walks away and I hear one of the little assholes say, "Damn! DD? I need to get my lady's tits done!" Now, he said it quietly, but my room was right next to the door so WTF!

Meanwhile, "helpful sales gal" brings me my ginormous DD bra. I try it on and it fits beautifully. I come out of the room and the little bastards are gone. "Helpful sales gal" then says to me, "I think you will still have some room to grow in that bra too."

Excuse me? Who said anything about growing any more? And THEN she says, "You will definitely need a new bra when you start lactating though."

GASP. How big am I going to get? What size does Dolly wear?

So then I call Ben to lament my situation and of course his response is, "Sweet, where's the camera?" Then he says, "What size comes after DD?" How the hell should I know! I didn't even know bras went past DD.

Feel free to share your similar story with me so I can feel better.

From: Natalie
To: Kim, Celeste
Sent: May 1

Holy crap. This is good stuff.

I know things have changed for me, and my bra might be too small because I'm dealing with deep red impressions from my underwire. I think I may go to Target and see what else fits, but after your account I'm not going to VS and getting measured. I guess all I can tell you is ... enjoy the next few months when you can be skinny with big boobs.

What size DOES come after DD?

The next time I see you, I'll try not to stare.

From: Celeste
To: Kim, Natalie
Sent: May 1

Wow! That is an impressive story ... and apparently you have impressive boobs. I can't wait to see them!

I hate to tell you that I am still wearing the same bras I was wearing before my husband did this awful thing to me. With Anna, I did grow ... one size up. When I was nursing, I was probably a large B cup ... and during pregnancy, I was an average B. Now I am actually probably a large A. Could wear a B but don't want to buy bras.

I wish I could join in your club, but, sadly, I cannot.

Delivering the Truth

At this point you may be thinking about the changes taking place with your own tatas and wondering what to expect if you haven't already experienced some changes in that area. We found this little factoid on a completely unreliable but fascinating website, so consider this: Breast changes are different for different women, but the range is from zero to 800 cc of volume per breast. The average is about 400 cc. For those of you who do not have your cc conversion chart in front of you, this means that 800 cc equals roughly 27 ounces, which is a little more than two cans of soda. Keep in mind that a woman's breast size can change up to 800 cc PER BREAST! We can only assume that our dear friend Kim is now carrying around four extra pop cans worth of boobage.

From: Natalie
To: Kim, Celeste
Sent: May 1

So I'm driving home from work today and I'm starving ... more hungry than I have ever been in my life. I decide to drive through Taco Bell. It's cheap and fast. I ordered four tacos and a giant nacho plate ... and I'm still not sure this is enough food.

As soon as the food is in my car, I cannot wait one second to eat it. I pull over in the parking lot and WOLF down a taco. There are other cars around me—I'm sure the families were shielding their children's eyes from seeing my barbaric eating habits. Who eats a taco in the car? Okay, I'm now ready to drive two minutes to my house.

I get home and head straight for the kitchen table. I don't even bother taking my coat off. I am sitting hunched over this enormous sack of food SHOVING it in my face. I cannot get the food in fast enough.

My poor, innocent husband comes around the corner to see what I was doing. He has to witness this poor state of affairs. I can't even look up at him because I'm so humiliated, but yet too starving to stop eating.

I yell at him, "I KNOW I'M DISGUSTING!"

He leans over to try and make eye contact with me, and all I can do is chew and cry. Yes, girls, I cried over tacos! He just looked at me like a deer in the headlights and then started laughing ... so I started laughing. I wiped the muck off my chin, cleared away the 800 taco wrappers and asked, "What's for dinner?"

From: Celeste
To: Kim, Natalie
Sent: May 2

Seriously, I think I might pee my pants. You should not have shared this story. You will never live it down. ☺

From: Kim
To: Natalie, Celeste
Sent: May 3

Have I mentioned the lovely dry heaving I am doing? I have yet to actually throw up but unfortunately ... when I least expect it, I start to dry heave. I have to constantly be sucking on something otherwise I just start retching. I was on the phone with Celeste the other day when I had to tell her to wait because it happened then. This is fun.

Delivering the Truth

To help with nausea, the Livestrong website suggests you may want to eat dry crackers before getting out of bed, smaller meals during the day, or take vitamin B6 (check with your doctor) or ginger. We recommend going straight for the large box of ginger snap cookies (with frosting).

From: Natalie
To: Celeste, Kim
Sent: May 3

I had a little cry this morning because I couldn't get my wedding ring on. Poor Brad just stared at me too afraid to move or speak. I just went into our closet and continued to get ready. It fit by the time I pulled into the parking lot at work.

We don't have our air conditioning on so I think I was just a little swollen this morning. However, I know there will soon be a time when my rings will no longer fit due to a combination of weight gain and swelling. I already feel fat and swollen everywhere, including my face. Sad times. And to add to it, I had a dream that I had the baby and his ears were all deformed. I remember looking at them to see if they were lower than his eyes ... and they were ... but then they were just kind of nubs of skin, not really ears.

Jeez. Add that to the list of "potentially horrible things that may happen."

This is really the first dream I had where I had a baby boy and I was looking at him. Maybe I should concentrate on that part.

From: Celeste
To: Kim, Natalie
Sent: May 3

I don't remember having dreams about what the baby looked like.

It was good to see you last night, and you look good. I don't think you look fat, and I don't think your face looks fat.

From: Natalie
To: Kim, Celeste
Sent: May 4

I was thinking about reading Brooke Shields's book about post-partum depression (PPD) after listening to the psychiatrist at work discussing baby blues, PPD, and psychosis with her students. Hopefully, I can avoid all that.

I'm trying to tell myself it's all attitude. Yeah, right. I think you are a kind, kind woman for telling me I look good and not fat. I weighed myself this morning. Why do I do that? It's never good news. I have never been so motivated to go to the gym in all my life! I hope this motivation will stick through my maternity leave so I can wear my old clothes again.

I think you look the same. Skinny Ass Snodgrass. No gut, no flab, no belly. You are delusional ... which, of course, I appreciate.

From: Kim
To: Natalie, Celeste
Sent: May 4

IT'S A GIRL! Ultrasound results were great! Ben and I are so excited because we *really* wanted a girl. Ben saw before I did that it was a girl and he was all teary. It was cool.

From: Natalie
To: Kim, Celeste
Sent: May 4

Congratulations! Now we just need to convince Celeste to find out what she is having!

From: Celeste
To: Kim, Natalie
Sent: May 4

That is awesome! Since Natalie is having a boy, your two babies can hook up!

 From: Natalie
To: Kim, Celeste
Sent: May 8

Jeez. One more thing to add to the list. I was totally off caffeine, but now I have one soda a day at lunch. I hope that is not enough to give my kid withdrawal headaches after birth. Crap. I didn't think of that. Oh, well, I need to stay awake at work and I DRAG after lunch.

 From: Kim
To: Natalie, Celeste
Sent: May 8

I spoke with a woman who runs a pregnancy yoga class. I remember Natalie telling me about a yoga class she attended where the instructor was always touching the women's bellies. So I asked this teacher if she was a freaky baby person and she said no.

Anyone want to try it?

From: Natalie
To: Kim, Celeste
Sent: May 8

Did you ask about primal moaning? I went to a prenatal yoga class a month ago and they did this primal moaning thing ... I am not a primal moaning type of girl. As long as this issue has been addressed, I think I could get into the four-week session.

From: Celeste
To: Kim, Natalie
Sent: May 8

Count me in!

From: Celeste
To: Kim, Natalie
Sent: May 8

My quad screen results are normal.

Good thing: only need to worry about placental abruption, club feet, gastroschisis, spina bifida, and any other nongenetic malformations.

Bad thing: since the results are normal, there is no need to see the perinatologist I love. I told the nurse (who knows I am a bit paranoid): "Oh, good, I guess I don't need to be a freak about *that* then," and she said, "Yes, Celeste, nothing bad is happening this week."

It is so nice to be understood ...

Dr. Bob says

A quad screen is a screening blood test that is done in the second trimester (typically between fifteen and twenty weeks estimated gestational age or EGA). It is a test that looks at four substances in a mother's blood. Based on the levels of those four substances, the test can give a risk for certain birth defects and chromosomal problems. It does not diagnose (say yes or no), it only gives a risk. It looks for things like Down syndrome and spina bifida. There are other prenatal screening tests as well.

Delivering the Truth

You may find yourself in our shoes. Motherhood for us started the moment we knew we were pregnant. We started worrying about all kinds of obscure and random medical problems that our children might be afflicted with, and we weren't afraid to voice our paranoia. Prenatal blood tests and ultrasounds helped squelch some of our fears, but heightened others or created new fears altogether.

From: Natalie
To: Celeste, Kim
Sent: May 8

That is great about the quad screen! I suppose now is as good a time as any to tell you guys that we had an abnormal one. We have a 1 in 69 chance of having a baby with Down. We've been seeing a perinatologist. After an ultrasound, he said my baby has a 2 percent chance of having Down. He has a "soft marker" for Down, which is a narrowed kidney duct.

All of this is really overwhelming and I'm just not ready to talk about it. I guess I just thought I'd let you guys know what is going on.

From: Celeste
To: Kim, Natalie
Sent: May 8

Wow. I'm glad you told us. We'll be here when you're ready.

From: Kim
To: Celeste, Natalie
Sent: May 8

I second that. We are always available for ice cream therapy.

From: Celeste
To: Kim, Natalie
Sent: May 8

I need to walk a bunch. I am getting outside to walk today or walking on the treadmill. My ass is starting to hang down to the back of my knees.

I am getting caffeine headaches every day. I always give in and drink at least a half can of Diet Mountain Dew. I am sure I am going to have a baby who has caffeine headaches when he/she is born. Won't that be fun to deal with?

Okay, I am off to do some work and then either get outside and walk or get on the treadmill.

Dr. Bob says

Exercise in pregnancy is a very common question. In general, in the absence of medical or obstetrical complications, thirty minutes or more of exercise a day is recommended. Avoid activities that have a risk of falling or abdominal trauma. Exercise in pregnancy has also been found to be beneficial in gestational diabetes not only in prevention, but also as adjunct treatment. Exercise helps if you have gestational diabetes, not only to prevent it but as an additional treatment if you do develop it.

Water exercise is often enjoyed quite a bit, other than the bathing suit issues, because it takes the effect of gravity off pregnant women. It should be noted that scuba diving should be avoided due to risk of decompression sickness of the fetus. As always, discuss exercise plans and routines with your health care provider.

From: Natalie
To: Kim, Celeste
Sent: May 9

I'm drinking my glucola as I type. It's just like sugary orange Sunkist ... not bad. I have my lab draw at 3:15, so I'm about to hit the road here pretty quick.

Dr. Bob says

Diabetic screening is a favorite of all women. A huge sugar bolus and then a blood draw an hour later. It is especially enjoyable to those having nausea and vomiting during pregnancy. The gold standard for the sugar bolus is a glucola drink. There are various flavors. There is some data that has looked at other options than the glucola drink such as jelly beans or candy bars. Although there is some data to support these alternatives, we docs traditionally enjoy the torture of the glucola drink.

From: Natalie
To: Kim, Celeste
Sent: May 10

My appointment went well. The nurse had to stick me twice ... she was mad at herself. I really didn't care. My doctor was trying to listen to the heartbeat as well as ask me social-worky questions about one of his patients. I was trying to be quiet to hear the heartbeat.

So my glucose results will be back on Thursday. Since I woke up I've had an achy pain that throbs in my ribs. Should I be worried about this? Do I have a placental abruption? I did stretch the other day and felt something pull. I'm a freak. Of course I went to the doctor yesterday and everything was fine.

No bleeding or loss of fluid. I would rate the pain as a three or four out of ten. Maybe it's just a stretching of the uterus/ ligaments pain.

Dr. Bob says

Placental abruption is when the placenta partially or completely separates from the uterine wall prior to the delivery of the baby. Typically, the hallmark of an abruption is painful third trimester vaginal bleeding. It is an uncommon event occurring in only about 1 percent of pregnancies, but can be associated with significant maternal and baby problems. If you have any bleeding, you need to notify your health care provider.

From: Celeste
To: Kim, Natalie
Sent: May 10

I love that you are a freak.

I think the pain that is most concerning is contractions ... and that is when there is a tightening of the belly—the entire belly. Or intense back pain that goes away and comes back.

You probably don't have an abruption. But I am glad you are paranoid about it. ☺ I am still just paranoid that the baby is dead and I have no symptoms.

Natalie, are you seeing the doctor every two weeks yet?

My doctor told me that he could just have everyone eat a king-sized Snickers bar instead of drinking the orange Sunkist for the glucose test—same amount of sugar. I voted for the Snickers.

From: Kim
To: Natalie, Celeste
Sent: May 10

A Snickers bar!? What the hell are they making us drink this orange crap for! What about Reese's Peanut Butter Cups?

From: Natalie
To: Kim, Celeste
Sent: May 10

Yes, I'm a freak. The pain has subsided for now. Hopefully forever. It wasn't all-over belly or back pain, it was a specific region ... so no contractions. Of course I've gone to the bathroom like fifty times today to check for blood.

Yes, every day I think the baby is dead. It would be better if we could just walk around with fetal monitors strapped to us. That would make me feel much better. I still need a few shirts. I could always use more pants but I'm refusing to buy any more. I'm just going to wear ugly clothes for a while longer.

I start doctor visits every two weeks now. It's a hell of a lot of visits. He told me yesterday, "So, Celeste tells me that you and she are 'psycho' and that I would be concerned with your conversations."

I just laughed and told him that yes, we do talk about terrible things that could happen to us or our babies and that we have working at the hospital to thank for that.

He just smiled and shook his head. You know why? Because he can't guarantee that everything is going to be okay. I'm sure he's just happy to have patients that are compliant and on time. So, zip it, Doc.

Damn! I wish I would have known about the king-sized Snickers ... that would have been much more enjoyable. I am eating less now. My stomach doesn't feel like it can hold much food anymore ... it's squished. Hopefully this will curb the extreme weight gain. What goes on must come off. I think we are going to pick out baby furniture and bedding this weekend. Then I want to register ... I don't know if Brad will be up for that or not. I just want to get on it. I want to move all the crap out of that bedroom and paint. Is this nesting or just wanting to have a place for the kid to sleep?

Today I'm telling people we are choosing between the names Merl and Harold. Personally, I prefer Merl. Lots of strange sideways looks going around.

Are you telling your names? Our name is pretty locked down (first and middle) ... I hope it's not the same as someone else's.

From: Kim
To: Natalie, Celeste
Sent: May 10

Ben and I learned the hard way not to share names. We told my parents we are considering Joaquin and that did not go over well. Something to do with an old cowboy show. Kelly Ripa named her son Joaquin, and I adore her, so how could we go wrong with that name?

We are now waiting to share the name until after the birth. People seem to reserve their opinion if the name is already on the birth certificate.

From: Natalie
To: Kim, Celeste
Sent: May 10

Got my results from the glucose test. My first good lab result!

They said they wouldn't call until tomorrow ... but she left a message for me today ... so of course I was just sure I have gestational diabetes ... but I don't.

Good news.

From: Natalie
To: Kim, Celeste
Sent: May 11

This is weird ... when I was at the doctor's office on Tuesday I was twenty-eight weeks exactly. They had me at twenty-seven and something. Shouldn't they be on top of this?

Yes, I'm a freak. Deep breaths.

Also, smells are driving me crazy again. I wore lotion yesterday that I've been wearing for a few months and thought I was going to gag. This morning I opened a new thing of deodorant and again I think I'm going to die. So off to the store to buy everything unscented again. Hello third trimester!

From: Celeste
To: Kim, Natalie
Sent: May 11

Ya know, according to my wheel, the nurse had me at the wrong dates too. But maybe she just has a wheel that is difficult to read the little dashes ... they are hard to read if you are blind like me.

Yea on your glucose test! I can't imagine how shitty it would be to have gestational diabetes!

I look pregnant today, and smells are starting to bother me too. John's diesel is horrible—and we were in his truck the other day and I suddenly said, "What is that horrible smell?" and he said the only thing he could smell was his windshield washer fluid.

I drank two regular fountain cokes today. I think my child is probably high.

Delivering the Truth

Pregnant women usually experience a heightened sense of smell during pregnancy. This is the body's way of protecting a pregnant woman from foods that are unsafe for the fetus.

 From: Natalie
To: Kim, Celeste
Sent: May 11

Damn, you are funny. I hope the nurse is just blind. No need to be pregnant three days longer than I need to be.

Yes, no gestational diabetes, so keep the sugar and carbs coming.

I had a Diet 7UP today with Splenda in it so I'm sure my kid is growing an extra appendage.

From: Natalie
To: Celeste, Kim
Sent: May 16

I just got back from one of my units in the hospital where psycho secretary greeted me with "Hi, Fat Girl." That woman obviously doesn't mind being judo chopped in the throat!

From: Celeste
To: Kim, Natalie
Sent: May 16

Who in their right mind would call a pregnant woman fat? Oh My God. That is amazing to me. I saw a shirt at a maternity boutique that says "Not fat, pregnant." You should wear that.

Delivering the Truth

In *What to Expect When You're Expecting*, it is recommended that the average woman gain between 25 to 35 pounds. We found this statement slightly amusing as collectively we gained 150 pounds.

From: Kim
To: Natalie, Celeste
Sent: May 16

Is everyone still up for yoga? I plan to call the gal tomorrow or Thursday to sign us up. My neighbor walked by and said he was glad he didn't have the biggest gut in the neighborhood anymore. I looked around to see who he was talking to.

 From: Celeste
To: Natalie, Kim
Sent: May 16

You are kidding, right? Who says that kind of stuff?
Yoga—count me in! My beer belly and wide ass/saddle bags are really making me nuts!

 From: Kim
To: Natalie, Celeste
Sent: May 17

Oh please. At least you aren't hauling around a set of Double D's!

 From: Natalie
To: Kim, Celeste
Sent: May 19

Rule #1: No pointing and laughing at Natalie's enormous body.

Rule #2: No commenting on the extreme whiteness of my skin.

Rule #3: If I pass out from fatigue ... let me lie there until the class is over.

Hey, by the way, what is that book you got that helps you get your babies into a sleep pattern? I'm trying to be prepared.

Delivering the Truth

You will be asked this question several million times after you deliver: "Is he sleeping through the night yet?" Sleeping through the night means different things to all of us. It may be helpful to know that between three and six months most babies will generally sleep between five and six hours and this is "sleeping through the night" by some experts' standards, maybe people who never had newborns. So if your baby goes to sleep at 8:00 p.m. you can expect him to wake up around 1:00 or 2:00 a.m. and gleefully state that, yes, he is sleeping through the night!

From: Celeste
To: Natalie, Kim
Sent: May 22

I woke up at 4 a.m. with the WORST heartburn ever. I woke John up and told him I thought I might die. He said to eat some pretzels. We didn't have any Tums or anything, so I ate pretzels and drank some water and then got every pillow in the house and tried to fall back asleep sitting up. Not very comfortable, but the heartburn did go away.

Of course, first thing this morning, I went to Target and got a bucket load of Tums.

I will look and see if I can find the name of the sleeping baby book—I know I wrote it down somewhere. I will let you know.

From: Natalie
To: Celeste, Kim
Sent: May 22

I caught sight of my rear end in the mirror during some bending over point in the class and thought I might pass out. Man, I wish it wasn't Sunday at 4 p.m. That is my only hang up (besides sweating and feeling like a pile in the class).

I feel good today ... not sore at all. We have the giant barrel of Tums also. Sometimes even brushing my teeth gives me heartburn. I usually only have to take them one or two times a week.

We cemented the name last night ... so I think it's becoming real now.

From: Natalie
To: Celeste, Kim
Sent: May 24

So this kid is not breech. He is head down. The doctor said he can still flip but he's in a good position right now. I waited an hour in the lobby to see my doctor for about a minute and a half. Good times. I do think it's funny that he can push around on your stomach and knows what the heck he is feeling. Weird ... but the baby is still alive ... good news.

Dr. Bob says

Breech refers to a baby's presentation or how the baby is lying. Breech is when the butt or feet are closest to the cervix. Breech is not uncommon early in pregnancy. About a third of babies are breech at sixteen to twenty weeks. About 20 to 25 percent are breech at twenty-eight weeks, and about 5 to 10 percent at thirty-two weeks. At birth about 3 percent are breech.

Typically breech babies are delivered by cesarean section today. There are options to try and turn a baby from breech (butt down) to vertex (head down) in the latter part of the third trimester. There are different types of breech: frank (pike position), complete (cannonball positions), or footling (one or both legs and feet extended down). Bottom line, most breech babies will turn on their own, and it can happen up to the last day.

From: Celeste
To: Natalie, Kim
Sent: May 24

Well, that is good news! Let's just hope that the little guy flips the right way when he does flip. Isn't it strange that he can tell the position of the kid without an ultrasound? I swear he could just tell by looking at me that I was still breech every time he saw me when I was pregnant with Anna. Anyway, I have my ultrasound on Tuesday—diagnosis time!

I am sitting outside in the back yard with my laptop and work and getting ready to write a report while Anna is napping. Gotta love laptops and wireless Internet!

From: Natalie
To: Celeste, Kim
Sent: May 24

Yep, I hope he just flips his legs around ... not his head! Diagnosis time is a good time. I have one last ultrasound with the perinatologist on the 19th and that is probably the last look we'll get until he's really here.

Last night we had the conversation of what if he is born with Down syndrome. We made some really selfish but honest statements that needed to be said out loud ... prior to delivery ... which are probably normal ... but I think that is how it has to be. We need to mentally prepare for the "what if's." I keep telling myself it's just a 2 percent chance. That is so tiny ... but still ... I'm a freak.

Yeah, your office space sounds a little nicer than mine.

 From: Kim
To: Natalie, Celeste
Sent: May 24

Your ultrasound will be fine and your little man will be too! Good for you and Brad for having an honest chat about the "what ifs." If you can't do this with your spouse, then you shouldn't be married, right?

By the way, Celeste, what do you wash baby clothes in? Are you supposed to wash them all before the baby wears them? Do you buy the special baby stuff or what? What if you get all prepared and wash the clothes and then the baby doesn't wear them? I really don't want to have to do any more laundry than necessary and, frankly, this all sounds like a PITA anyway.

From: Natalie
To: Celeste, Kim
Sent: May 28

Celeste, let us know how your MD appointment goes. Are you sure you don't want to peek and find out for sure if it's a boy?

From: Celeste
To: Natalie, Kim
Sent: May 28

I'll let you know after my appointment how it goes—but, no, sorry, no peeking!

As for the specialized baby laundry detergent. Don't bother. Use either Cheer Free or All Free & Clear. They are the same things. You do need to use something without dye in it though. Babies will break out from a harsh detergent. If your baby has sensitive skin, you need to wash your clothes in it also since his head/face will be touching your clothes.

Frankly, it is easier if you are all using the same detergent because then you don't have to separate baby clothes and adult clothes. That is a pain. Just try not to lose any of the tiny baby socks when you wash all your clothes together (like static electricity causing one to get stuck inside your husband's pants and then falling out at work).

From: Natalie
To: Celeste, Kim
Sent: May 28

We went to a lake house on Saturday. It was SO nice and relaxing. I could certainly get used to that life. There was one other pregnant lady and two others that had newborns ... so it was A LOT of baby talk. I felt very out of place because the moms seemed to know exactly what their baby needed.

And the pregnant lady knew what position her baby was in just by feeling (she's due two days before me) and she was talking about hiccups. I felt very disconnected. She was also wearing a swimming suit while I was sweating my ass off in denim capris and a tank top (feeling extremely NAKED).

So now I'm freaked out that I'm not going to know how to take care of this guy. How much and how often do you even feed them? Holy crap. Celeste, did you ever go through this?

At least we got the room done and all the furniture in there. It's very clean so I have closed the door and can leave it alone— for a while anyway.

 From: Celeste
To: Natalie, Kim
Sent: May 28

I just have a minute—

My motto: Fake it 'til you make it.

Confide in one of the nurses you trust that you don't know shit and need Baby Care 101 when you and Brad come in to deliver. Tell them (if it makes you feel better) that you have a basic idea, but Brad is beyond clueless, which he is, so that isn't a lie. They understand and will do lots of education. And the bath—they will give you a bath demo. I asked one of the nurses to give the bath demo when everyone was there (John, mom, etc.), that way everyone learned at the same time and I didn't feel like the fool.

Okay, gotta run. I will email after the ultrasound!

Delivering the Truth

Of course, all of these questions could have been easily answered in a prenatal class ... had we gone.

From: Celeste
To: Kim, Natalie
Sent: May 29

So everything went well at my ultrasound yesterday. Since my doc already knows that I am a total freak, he walked me through everything and explained all the little details. I am feeling pretty good about the whole thing and for the moment am not fearful that this baby has some obscure diagnosis. And no, we didn't peek!

From: Kim
To: Natalie, Celeste
Sent: May 29

I am glad your ultrasound went well! Seriously, Celeste, you know how I hate it when people don't find out the gender. You must be doing this to annoy me as opposed to relishing the idea of an awesome surprise in twenty or so weeks. I'm not sure our friendship can continue on like this ...

From: Natalie
To: Celeste, Kim
Sent: May 29

I'm glad that your ultrasound went well. It's nice to know all the parts are where they should be. Now the only thing you have to worry about is ambiguous genitalia ... ☺

Delivering the Truth

In an unofficial poll we found that 68 percent of respondents learned the gender of their child prior to birth.

Dr. Bob says

Only the weak ones who need immediate gratification find out the gender of their child before birth. Obviously most are weak. However, there are those of us with willpower. ☺

From: Natalie
To: Celeste, Kim
Sent: May 30

Hair appointment made, day saved. I can't have gray hair for my baby shower. JEEZ! I need a pedicure too. And a new outfit to wear for the shower.

A girl at work told me that you can't get pedicures while you are pregnant because it can cause preterm labor. At this point, I think I'm nearly okay with that. ☺ Although you aren't supposed to color your hair either. And this weekend I went to a tanning salon and did that spray tan thing. Those are some really good fumes for the kiddo. Hopefully he doesn't come out glowing or anything.

One of the case managers said, "Wow Natalie ... you really popped out this weekend. Had you noticed that?" What? The enormous gut that hangs over my pants and gets to every location ten minutes before I do? NO, I HADN'T NOTICED!!

Dr. Bob says

Coloring your hair during pregnancy, I must admit that I know nothing about this. Personally, as a male, I am just happy to still have mine, whatever color it is becoming.

From a pregnancy standpoint, it is an extremely common and important question to many pregnant ladies. There is very little data available and most data and evidence is observation or surveillance data. It would appear to be safe. OTIS (The Organization of Teratology Information Services), which gives information about risks for birth defects, does not report an increased risk.

With this said, it is always wise to try and wait until the first trimester has been completed (that is when the organs are forming). Also, the chemicals used are not absorbed into the body through the hair, but a very small amount is absorbed through skin. Thus, wear gloves and do not leave it on the scalp any longer than necessary to reduce exposure.

But in summary, coloring your hair does not appear to significantly increase the risk of birth defects or problems.

From: Natalie
To: Celeste, Kim
Sent: May 31

So I'm totally concentrating on movements today. Too bad he's packed in there like a sardine and not moving very much. Maybe I should get a Mountain Dew.

From: Celeste
To: Natalie, Kim
Sent: May 31

Yes, get a Mountain Dew and then start poking but not hard enough to cause a placental abruption. ☺

Have I told you about Simply Lemonade? That is quite possibly the best drink ever created. They also make Simply Limeade, which I am tempted to try, but Simply Cherry–Limeade would be the ultimate. I haven't seen that at the store yet.

From: Kim
To: Celeste, Natalie
Sent: May 31

Nat, why don't you just start an IV of Mountain Dew?

Dr. Bob says

Fetal movements. What's normal? Quickening, or first sensation of baby's movement, typically occurs at about eighteen to twenty weeks gestation. It may be slightly earlier in moms who have had babies prior. Generally, they initially feel like little flutters or gas bubbles. These movements steadily become stronger and more intense, resulting sometimes in significant discomfort for mom. It is not uncommon later in pregnancy to actually see movements of baby causing mom's belly to move.

In the later third trimester the movements can be reported to change again, sometimes becoming less vigorous or violent. However, it is important to note that the baby should continue to move throughout pregnancy. Discuss this with your health care provider.

June

From: Celeste
To: Natalie, Kim
Sent: June 4

So remember when I had my torn retina last year? Well, this morning, I had the same thing happen to me—bright white floaties.

I called the doctor and I have to go in tomorrow morning at 9:00 a.m. Until then, I can't lift anything, bend over, etc. I guess that means no laundry today. ☺ But what a pain in the ass. I was hoping to go to yoga tonight and now I can't. I really don't want to have another torn retina. The laser surgery, although by comparison, not bad—sucked. I think he will have to give me a bit of Xanax this time around.

Sometimes I think that maybe I should go on the "Anna diet" and eat the same portions/things she eats. Then I would be skinny. She is healthy, so I could be healthy too on her diet, right? Is this delusional?

Okay, I am off to relax and try not to strain my eyes and tear my retina even further than it already is ... if it is torn. Natalie, have fun shopping for a cute outfit for the shower. I can't wait to see what you come up with! I will probably have to borrow it sooner rather than later since I am now officially a showing pregnant lady. And I SWEAR that some maternity clothes shrink in the wash.

Delivering the Truth

We all agree that maternity clothes are getting better throughout the years. However, with that fashion forward approach comes a larger price tag. We all want to look cute but no one wants to spend a fortune on clothes that you will only wear for a short time.

This is where girlfriends unite and share the "giant lady clothes" amongst each other. Ask your friends if you can borrow their maternity clothes and share yours. It saves a ton of money. Also, this will make you feel better when your maternity clothes suddenly seem to shrink in the washer and dryer.

Also, here's a nice tidbit—your biggest maternity clothes will likely not even fit you in your last few weeks. Maternity clothes have one job—and one job only—to cover your enormous body. When they fail to do the job, it is a sad, sad day. The silver lining here is that at this stage in the game you really don't give a shit.

From: Natalie
To: Celeste, Kim
Sent: June 5

Torn retina ... not good. Didn't your doc say it was guaranteed to happen again? Let me know how your appointment goes and if you can see the keyboard or your phone.

I decided against yoga. I am eight weeks out from the due date ... and I am having a lot of groin and back pain. Bending over is becoming a real problem. Any suggestions for relief?

I washed all the clothes we have in regular detergent ... oh well. I'll do the next batch in the right stuff. I hope he doesn't have sensitive skin. Actually, knowing that I am now a freak I'll probably wash them again. The problem is Brad likes really strong smelling detergent and he likes to use about half a box of dryer sheets. I'll have to give him a little talking to. Thanks for the info.

I would like to go on a kid diet, too. My niece is so skinny and she eats less than half of her food and always passes on chips or only eats a few fries. I agree, go on the toddler/little kid diet. I look like I ate a toddler ...

As far as the cute shower outfit. No luck. I looked at all the major maternity clothing stores—the mediums are too small and the larges are way too big. I found a pair of capris ... but they are white and I fear white pants. So I have to take drastic measures. I'm going to go look at the specialty boutiques. I guess if I spend some cash on one good outfit, it is excusable.

I'll let you know how it goes. I hope I find something, otherwise I'll have to wear my weekend uniform ... denim capris and a maternity t-shirt.

Stay tuned (with your good eye).

From: Kim
To: Natalie, Celeste
Sent: June 5

You two are falling apart on me! I fear I may be the last one standing when this is all said and done!

Celeste, have I told you that you have some jacked-up eyes?! Do I have to take you to your appointment again? I'm going to start charging you cab fare.

 From: Celeste
To: Natalie, Kim
Sent: June 5

Do different positions help with the back and groin pain? Like lying on the floor with your legs against the wall like we did at yoga? What about on your hands and knees belly hanging down—takes the pressure off the back. What does your chiropractor say?

I am back from the eye doctor and do not have another torn retina, thank God! He said that every time I see those flashing lights, I need to come in and get checked out ... because you never know.

I am really tired today. I don't know if I was just a stress basket yesterday and didn't get good sleep last night or what, but I could really use a nap.

I think you may have some luck at Gap Maternity. They had some cute stuff that was pretty summery for your shower. Make sure if it's cotton that you get it a little bit big because it shrinks! And if you are going to wear the jean capris, let me know. I don't want to wear a skirt if you are wearing capris!

From: Natalie
To: Celeste, Kim
Sent: June 5

Different positions don't really help. When I sleep at night with the body pillow, I wake up with a big pain in my stomach ... so I roll over and about die. I'm not sure what organ I'm squishing ... but it doesn't like it.

I have tried the feet up against the wall position at home. I have to bend my legs now. Also, modified child's pose [a yoga position] is getting more difficult. I've tried to sit criss-cross on the floor and then rest my head on the bed. That seems to help after about ten minutes. My chiropractor just says, "Yep, it's because of all the stress on your body."

Good on the intact retina. Always a good thing.

I'll check out the boutique places and Gap Maternity. I will not be wearing my denim capris ... that would be worst-case scenario. I wanted to dress up a bit. My sister says I have to surrender about the ankle/cankle situation. I will be elevating my legs a lot before the shower though ... so they can at least be in sort of good shape.

Delivering the Truth

Let's talk pain in general. Natalie and Kim seemed to experience odd pains during their pregnancies. We found that our bodies just started falling apart at various gestations. You may find that you experience pain in random places only to learn from your doctor that "it's just a part of pregnancy."

From: Natalie
To: Celeste, Kim
Sent: June 6

I am sitting at work and my chronic heartburn has turned to nausea ... gross. I want to go home.

This must be the whining stage. Who knew I'd be so good at it? (This is a rhetorical question ... no need to answer so loudly!)

 From: Celeste
To: Natalie, Kim
Sent: June 6

Nausea? Really? That sucks. I mean, nausea sucks normally, but when you are fifteen months pregnant, that is even worse.

 From: Natalie
To: Celeste, Kim
Sent: June 6

After suffering a few days in the middle of summer with a broken air conditioner, I am happy to report it is FREEZING in our house! I got to sleep with a blanket on ... our dogs are actually up and moving around and not lying half dead on the floor. I love modern technology.

Maybe I'll be a nicer person now ... nah ... probably not.

Oh, and I found a dress. I originally didn't look at dresses ... but I went back and found one that I can wear to both showers and hopefully both weddings (mid-July). It's light blue, and I bought a brown cardigan to go over it. Hope it will still fit in July.

From: Celeste
To: Natalie, Kim
Sent: June 8

I know I'm being stupid. My air conditioner broke and the HVAC guy just left. We can't repair it—we need a whole new unit.

The guy walked out of my house and I started crying. I can't even think about it without crying again.

Thank you for listening to my hormonal vent.

From: Natalie
To: Kim, Celeste
Sent: June 8

This sounds like an event of Taco Bell proportions. But ... mentioning that, I won't comment on it further. It sucks.

From: Kim
To: Natalie, Celeste
Sent: June 8

I am sorry, but nothing will make me laugh like Natalie buying out all the food at Taco Bell and then wolfing it down in front of her husband who was probably thinking, "Isn't that sweet that she brought me something to eat too," and then realizing that his hand had been gnawed off after it was mistaken for a burrito that he had been reaching for.

From: Natalie
To: Kim, Celeste
Sent: June 8

Okay, listen. The Taco Bell incident was of epic proportions ... you are right. All other humans in the vicinity were in danger. At least Brad has enough sense not to mention it or share the joke with his buddies (in my presence anyway). I am dangerous when I'm hungry.

There was another incident where I was out to brunch with my sister, Angie, and two girlfriends. I bought a monster cookie to nibble on while I was waiting for my little breakfast sandwich to be prepared. My sister reached across the table and broke off a chunk of it and ate it. I stared at her in disbelief.

I said, "Did you honestly just take food from a pregnant woman?" I was not joking. I was pissed.

She apologized profusely and said she'd buy me another one ... and then I felt terrible. I am apparently a mean and terrible person when hungry. Let this be a warning to you both.

 From: Kim
To: Natalie, Celeste
Sent: June 8

Ben knows that when I say, "I'm getting kind of hungry," that really means, "Find the nearest food place and get me something to eat as quickly as possible or die trying."

From: Natalie
To: Kim, Celeste
Sent: June 8

Smart, smart man.

From: Celeste
To: Natalie, Kim
Sent: June 8

Okay, at least you made me laugh. Maybe in a few days I will believe you that this situation equates Taco Bell ... Oh, and the monster cookie incident.

Off to ease my emotional pain and suffering with banana bread ...

From: Natalie
To: Kim, Celeste
Sent: June 8

I had some banana bread this morning too, so I hope my leg cramps will go away. Is it a good time to mention that when I sit at my desk and chart, my stomach hits my thighs? It makes me puke a little bit in my mouth when I think about it. GROSS!

From: Kim
To: Natalie, Celeste
Sent: June 8

WTF, Celeste! Banana bread? Nothing eases one's pain like something from my favorite ice cream joint—Maggie Moo's!

Banana bread? Sheesh ... give me a break!

And, Natalie, honey, try having your boobs lie on your stomach. I look at Ben daily and ask him how he can live with me since I find myself disgusting. Please, God, don't let my boobs sag to my knees after this is all over.

Does it make you feel a little better if I tell you that someone asked my brother about how he felt about me being pregnant and he said (and I quote), "She's pregnant? I thought she was just eating a lot of Twinkies!"

Bastard.

Delivering the Truth

A note to the partners of the preggos. Your attitude can make or break a mood swing. Now is the time to lie to your wife or partner. Here are our recommendations. Start and end every sentence with these comments:

—I think you look so beautiful right now!

—I can't even tell you are pregnant from behind!

—You look like a stomach on a stick!

—No, there's no swelling in your ankles. None at all.

—You look like you're only five months not eight.

—Supermodels are overrated. Who needs them?

From: Celeste
To: Natalie, Kim
Sent: June 8

Apparently I don't have money to buy Maggie Moo's ice cream because I am spending it all on a new HVAC unit ... so I have to eat something that I already have in the house.

From: Kim
To: Celeste, Natalie
Sent: June 8

I understand completely and as your friend will not make any comments about the $175 pair of maternity jeans you told me you bought the other day. ☺

From: Natalie
To: Kim, Celeste
Sent: June 8

Neither will I ... HOLY CRAP!! Um ...

From: Celeste
To: Natalie, Kim
Sent: June 8

Which were returned and exchanged for two pairs of capri pants, and I still have $50 left over at the store to spend on a desperate day. This is why I keep tags on everything I purchase on my "I feel fat and I have low self-esteem and buying something outrageous will make me feel better" days ...

So, you are right, my friend, no need to comment. ☺

From: Kim
To: Celeste, Natalie
Sent: June 8

So then $50 may be enough to go to Maggie Moo's! I mean, it wouldn't be enough for me but perhaps if you have a punch card and could get one cone for free then you could make do with only $50. Think about it ... banana bread or Maggie Moo's?

From: Celeste
To: Natalie, Kim
Sent: June 8

Why do you guys keep emailing me? Do you have nothing better to do? Because of the constant emails, I have been unable to even make it down the stairs to eat the stupid banana bread. I haven't had one glass of water today and I need to go get Anna.

So go pretend like you have a life or something and quit bugging me!

From: Celeste
To: Natalie, Kim
Sent: June 9

I got a pedicure to ease my emotional pain. I highly recommend it during pregnancy. ☺

From: Natalie
To: Celeste, Kim
Sent: June 9

I'll have to check out the pedicure. I might even break down and try the pregnancy massage ... if nothing else I can lie on my stomach for an hour. See you gals tomorrow at my baby shower!

From: Natalie
To: Kim, Celeste
Sent: June 16

I think I have carpal tunnel. My doctor said we could talk about it more at my appointment next week, but it sounds like that is what I have. To top it off, it doesn't go away until eight to twelve weeks after delivery ... JOY! I woke up this morning and could barely get my hands to make a fist. Then they continue to be numb and clumsy all day. I asked Brad to squeeze my hands last night, and he said the skin and joints feel tight.

I'm thinking amputation.

I'm tired, swollen, and grouchy. I'll stop griping now.

From: Celeste
To: Natalie, Kim
Sent: June 16

Wow—That sucks! How are you supposed to pick up a baby when you can't feel your hands? Ah, the joys of pregnancy ...

 From: Natalie
To: Celeste, Kim
Sent: June 16

I think I'm going to have to use the Hoyer lift to move the kid ... the same lift that I'm using now to get me out of bed. Right now it's really just my fingers. I hope it won't move on down to my wrists.

 From: Natalie
To: Celeste, Kim
Sent: June 19

Is it wrong that I'm chugging diet soda before my ultrasound so I can see my kid squirm around on the ultrasound instead of the boring ole sleep mode.

He won't have ADHD or be so jittery that he wraps himself in the cord ... right??

From: Celeste
To: Natalie, Kim
Sent: June 19

Right. No cord wrapping going on with your kid. Now that you are admitting it, I will admit it too: Diet Mountain Dew about one hour before the ultrasound. ☺ We are sick.

From: Kim
To: Celeste, Natalie
Sent: June 19

Dumb question ... when I am closer to delivery how will my MD know what position my kid is in? Do they know by feel or do I have another ultrasound? I thought I would only have one ...

From: Celeste
To: Kim, Natalie
Sent: June 19

If your doctor is as cool as mine, then he knows just by looking at you. Your doctor should be able to tell the position just by touching your belly and pushing (gently) around body parts. If there is a question, then they will ultrasound. I had about a million ultrasounds during those last few weeks at work in the hospital to see if Anna had flipped.

Of course, those were nurses and residents doing the ultrasounds. If my doc had been there, I would have never had the ultrasound. Every time I went into his office, he could tell me without hesitation.

Not a dumb question.

From: Kim
To: Celeste, Natalie
Sent: June 19

Great ... more prodding and poking. This is one reason why I wished I still worked at the hospital ... free ultrasounds!

From: Natalie
To: Celeste, Kim
Sent: June 19

My doctor poked around at my last appointment (thirty-two weeks) and told me the position. According to the ultrasound he was right on. Head down, butt and an arm under my ribs (good for rib pain and indigestion) and feet over in the middle of my left side. His face is facing up—but his body is lying on his side.

So he's in a good spot—he just needs to face down and move his back over a bit. No problem. The perinatologist said when I drop (yeah, right) he'll be in an appropriate position for delivery.

By the way, the ultrasound tech was not gentle. I swear I still have that probe thing embedded in my spleen. Okay, no ... I don't know where my spleen is but I know there is an ultrasound probe in it now. I think she was digging in to get a good picture of the face—bad idea. He looks like a ghost with black eye sockets and all shadowy—not worth it so much.

Not a dumb question, Kim, I wouldn't know that either unless I knew that my doctor just felt around for where the body parts were lying. So, thirty-four weeks now. My days of the noninvasive MD appointments are coming to an end very soon.

Delivering the Truth

Doctors do something that is called the Leopold's maneuver. They touch your belly in four specific areas to determine where the head and butt are located.

From: Kim
To: Celeste, Natalie
Sent: June 19

Hmmm ... that does not sound pleasant so I am going to keep my fingers crossed that I will have no need for any internal probing, spleen altering ultrasounds if that is how they do them. Glad to hear he is in the right position. How often do you feel him move now?

From: Natalie
To: Celeste, Kim
Sent: June 20

So we had "the appointment" yesterday with the perinatologist. I feel like I'm back at square one and we just got our results of the quad screen.

The good news is—it's still a boy and his head is down. He weighs approximately 4.6 pounds, which the doctor said if I deliver on my due date (which I won't) and they are exactly right about his weight (which they aren't) I can expect a baby in the low 7-pound range. He said everything looks good—good fluid, good growth, good movement, good organs. Great. I can handle that.

The only "off" thing was the femur measurement. He said the femur is measuring on the low end of the scale, which could be another "soft indicator" of Down syndrome. He said, "This could also be constitutional because you and Brad are not 6 feet tall." WTF? He said he would have a report typed up for my regular OB for my Tuesday appointment. He asked about the amniocentesis again. I can't make a decision these days so Brad said he's still comfortable with not doing it.

Then we hit the parking lot and freak out. WTF? I know the doctor is trained to look at the littlest things and in the grand scheme of things it's still a 2 percent chance of Down syndrome. We aren't going to do anything different but be sad sooner rather than later. But I just can't get over it now. I thought about it all last night and am up at 5:00 a.m. to email you and think about it some more.

Now Brad says if it was just up to him he'd probably do the amnio—just for the definitive answer. I guess I'll talk to my doctor about it at my appointment today. I'm really not jazzed about a needle in my stomach but then we would know for sure, we would have our answer, which is also scary. Denial is a good thing sometimes, you know?

I'll let you know about the amniocentesis. I wonder how that works—if they do it in the clinic or if you are admitted for observation or what. I'm not scared of rupturing anymore. A thirty-four-week baby wouldn't be in the NICU for much more than a week. I guess it's the answer that I'm scared of. I selfishly would just be crushed that the image of "the perfect fantasy child" would be gone and I would have to readjust my thinking.

I know all this is normal and it would be appropriate to be sad, but still. Okay, I think I'm done talking about this for now— no need to cry over something that hasn't happened yet, right? I'll let you know the decision.

From: Natalie
To: Celeste, Kim
Sent: June 21

I went to the doctor this morning and talked to him at length about the amnio, and I guess what I came away with is that I believe there is more than a slight risk that he has Down. We went over all my scans and compared them.

At my first ultrasound the femur length was like 26th percentile, 2nd ultrasound it was at the 12th percentile, and now it's at the 10th percentile. That also freaks me out. His other bones in his legs and arms are growing normally. My doctor said that he is at the 28th percentile overall for growth. That freaks me out. He said he doesn't worry about the overall growth unless it's below the 10th percentile.

In passing he threw out the word *acondroplagia* (dwarfism). I don't think he was speculating that he has dwarfism, but of course my brain grabs a hold of that as another thing to worry about.

So I told him I feel like I just need someone to tell me what to do. He said with my state of mind that I shouldn't do it. It's not going to matter. If he does have Down, he doesn't have a heart defect or anything so a specialist wouldn't need to be standing by. I will not be any more prepared for it today than I will be in six weeks.

He asked what Brad wants to do. I told him that Brad wants to do it. Then he said do it. So I left the office in total ambiguous limbo. I called Brad and freaked out and he said let's just do it and get it over with.

My doctor said we'd have the initial results in twenty-four hours and then the full genetic panel back in a week. He said he would do it at the office and told me to think about it and come back in a week. Brad had to go to softball last night and got home late so we didn't have a lot of time to chat about it. This morning

I just asked if anything had changed in his mind and he snapped at me and said he's not going to rehash it. Okay. Great.

So then I have to cry all the way to work. Of course I'm listening to that damn Beatles song, "Let It Be" ... probably the best music choice for the moment. This is what I've come up with. I believe that this kid has a real chance of having Down. I think if I know that before I deliver that I might not have the extra "umpf" needed to push him out (if I'm lucky enough not to have a c-section). That sounds terrible.

I am sad about this and then I kick my own ass about it for being selfish and sad about it. I guess that is where I'm at. I try to walk myself through the worst-case scenario. If he does have Down, I will just be really sad and feel bad that I failed and I know it's something I can learn to handle but I don't know if Brad can.

So, as of today, I'm not having the amnio ... for the very small reason of not having it still gives me the hope of having a healthy child without Down.

Make sense??

 From: Celeste
To: Natalie, Kim
Sent: June 21

You are making me cry.

I understand why you are not having the amnio. I also understand your need to hash it out over and over and over ...

Did your doctor say that he thinks there is more than a "slight risk" that he has Down? I think the femur thing would freak me out too and make me think the chances were higher than 2 percent. Your doctor is right in that he doesn't have a heart condition, which is awesome—but still.

When in doubt, listen to Paul McCartney and John Lennon. They know what to do ... I think "Let It Be" was a good song to listen to.

There is nothing you (or anyone) can do about the situation, just let it happen, finish your pregnancy, and look forward to the birth of your son.

And like Dori says in Finding Nemo, "Just keep swimming!"

From: Kim
To: Natalie, Celeste
Sent: June 21

This is way overwhelming and emotional. I don't know what to say. Why is it that women become mothers almost from the day of conception and the worrying begins? Hang in there girl ...

From: Natalie
To: Celeste, Kim
Sent: June 21

Well don't cry, Celeste, because then I'll cry and if we, the women of steel, are both crying at the same time, the Earth will stop spinning. ☺

I appreciate your emails and your careful thoughts. It means a lot to hear another person say, "I understand that ... "

He didn't say anything about there being more than a "slight risk" ... and the perinatologist said the risk is 2.5 to 3 percent rather than the original 2 percent. He said that the amnio would be 100 percent accurate for Trisomy 18 and 21 though. So it's still a slight risk ... low risk. The femur is just new information to me, and I know the perinatologist is trained to find the needle in the haystack. I agree, when in doubt listen to the Beatles. They have good advice. I will keep swimming, let it be, finish my pregnancy, and deliver my son.

Delivering the Truth

About 120,000 babies (1 in 33) in the United States are born each year with birth defects, according to the March of Dimes. That means there are a lot of very special children out there whose parents may have felt similar feelings as Natalie does during this time. Feelings of isolation and disappointment mixed with hope can be overwhelming and it is very important to seek support from those you trust.

From: Celeste
To: Natalie, Kim
Sent: June 21

Anna is supposed to be taking a nap and she is in her room singing the Mickey Mouse Club song. She is yelling (and when I say yelling, I really mean that I am surprised you can't hear her at work), "Yea Mickey, Yea Mickey, Yea Mickey Mouse Club!"

I just had a sandwich and about a hundred Cheetos for lunch ... healthy.

From: Natalie
To: Celeste, Kim
Sent: June 21

I did hear a faint bit of "Yea Mickey" earlier ... so that explains where it came from.

I've had two people ask me if I'm feeling okay today because I look "really swollen." Thanks.

It is 900 degrees outside and I've been running around today ... I also ate a big lunch so give me a break ... I'm growing a human here. My hands and feet are not abnormally swollen so I figure I'm okay.

Brad asked me to go to his softball tournament this weekend with him. It's in Bismarck, North Dakota, which is about eight and a half hours away ... um ... probably not. No need to deliver in Bismarck. Where the hell is Bismarck anyway?

From: Natalie
To: Celeste, Kim
Sent: June 26

It has happened. I became an evil bitch this morning and now I'm questioning my parental abilities. Here is the horrific tale:

We got a sprinkler system this weekend ... great, fine, whatever (we barely have grass to water these days). So this morning the dogs wake me up at 6:00 a.m. to go outside. I sleepwalk down the hall and let them out ... only to realize the sprinklers are on. I try to get them back in the house ... but no ... that becomes impossible. So I go about my business and have faith that my intelligent dogs will have the sense to stay away from the water and mud ... stay tuned.

My dogs come to the door SOAKING WET and COVERED IN MUD. Their feet are unrecognizable because they are just clods of juicy mud. I cuss and grumble for a while but then get to work. I get Austin first. He is patient and lets me scrub his feet until I'm satisfied. I'm getting pissed though because it is taking forever and I am now running late.

Then comes goofy Jackson. Poor dog. He is the worst of the two. I start to wipe his drenched coat ... then go to the feet. I just start on the first one when I realize that I need another towel. I command him to stay and threaten his life if he doesn't. He seems to understand me ... so I go five steps into the laundry room and who is behind me in stealth mode ... but JACKSON.

I scream and holler for him to get back on the rug. He gets spooked and starts running around the basement ... paws covered in more mud than I thought was on the planet. I grab his collar and try to drag his 140 pounds of dead weight back to the rug. No luck.

Now I'm screaming and cussing and nearly crying because I'm so late, and now dirty, and just overall pissed. He finally gets back onto the rug where I spend the next thirty minutes cleaning him up. I gazed at the carpet and just decided I'm going to have to do it when I got home.

Brad, of course, slept through this. He has no idea what I'm capable of. My poor dog, Jackson, may never forgive me.

To top it off ... I had to move into the granny undies (too much info I realize) and I'm more waddling than walking due to the extreme pain in my groin. I also stepped on the scale this morning and had a stroke.

What's new with you girls? Were you at the lake in your bikinis sipping virgin daiquiris all weekend?

From: Celeste
To: Natalie, Kim
Sent: June 27

I almost killed the cable installer guy yesterday. He showed up wearing nothing that identified him as the cable guy and driving his personal vehicle. Then, everything that was supposed to be done yesterday, he said, wasn't on his work order. How the hell would he even know if it was on his work order? He didn't have one single piece of paper with him when he showed up at my door!

Anyway, he told me that this was going to cost extra money, and he couldn't do the computer stuff—that I needed a "professional Internet installer" and that would cost another $300.

I told him that we ordered all of this when we called to set up the work ... he suggested I call the cable company. So I did. I talked to the woman John spoke with to set the whole thing up. And guess what? It was all on the work order including the "professional Internet install."

I really was going to blow his head off. He didn't know what he was doing when it came to most things. He called his boss who came out and did all of the Internet install and was nice and pleasant and checked all of the guy's work before he left.

The cable lady that I spoke to said that they go by a point system on the difficulty of a job, and our difficulty rating was "82." I told her the guy they sent out was a "20 point" guy.

Anyway, that is my bitching. Saw my doc today. All is well. I get to drink the orange crap for my next visit. Yeah.

Delivering the Truth

If you find yourself crying at Hallmark commercials, overreacting to benign comments from loved ones and complete strangers, thinking of strategic plans on how to save your unborn child from an alien invasion after watching a movie, then you too may have been slapped by the hormone stick.

From: Kim
To: Celeste, Natalie
Sent: June 27

I just got done drinking my orange crap. Now I start my every-two-week appointments. I have gained nineteen pounds. I can't decide if I am happy with that or not since I have three months left.

From: Natalie
To: Celeste, Kim
Sent: June 27

The orange crap is so enjoyable. I was sure I was diabetic but it's actually the one test that I passed. YAHOO! I think something weird is going on with my blood sugar though because I'm always thirsty and I've felt faint twice in the past week. I'll chat with my doc about it at my next appointment.

That is funny that you almost killed the cable guy. Ever since I've been pregnant I've been a freak about people at the door. I've lost my ability to be nice to door-to-door salespeople. I no longer tell them that our dogs are harmless. I am just trying to avoid being the lady that gets chopped up and some weirdo steals the baby. Irrational? Not me.

I feel for ya, Kim, with the every-two-week visits ... I'm up to weekly now. Who the hell has time to go to the MD once a week?

Oh, and at lunch it was "tell your horrible pregnancy loss story day" ... WTF people?

From: Kim
To: Natalie, Celeste
Sent: June 28

I understand about being chopped up in pieces. I have noticed an almost uncontrollable fear of riding in the car with Ben. He is a good driver but tends to be a little aggressive. I spend more time slamming my foot on my own imaginary brake pedal because I believe we are going to either crash or get hit. I am constantly checking the position of my seat belt.

From: Natalie
To: Celeste, Kim
Sent: June 28

This is the second night in a row that I've had to sleep on the couch in nearly the sitting position. I always try to lie down in bed but I get so nauseous I can't stand it. Last night I was up dry heaving. WTF?

Obviously my guts are squished to the max. I eat a small dinner as early as possible and then don't eat much (grapes or something) at about 8:00 p.m. or so and that is it. I need this kid to drop so I can start grouching about peeing my pants instead of barfing in bed.

Girls, how are you holding up? Kill any innocent cable men yet today, Celeste?

 From: Kim
To: Natalie, Celeste
Sent: June 28

I'm happy to reply that I kindly suggested my husband sleep in another room last night. Wisely, he did so which meant that I only woke up at 1:15 to pee and then slept peacefully the entire night. I am refreshed this morning. It is amazing how one feels when they aren't woken up five times a night.

Interestingly as well, I have experienced no hormonal breakdowns or episodes of rage. I passed my glucose test and now my only complaint is twice a month MD visits.

On another and more delicate note (this is not for the squeamish or faint of heart). I'm the type of girl who likes to keep things, shall we say, neat and trimmed looking. I typically get a bikini wax. I realized yesterday that I can no longer see anything to effectively trim the nether regions. I have a huge fear of going in to deliver and looking like wolf puss, wild and unruly. Am I the only one with these concerns? If so, what is your plan of attack?

From: Natalie
To: Kim, Celeste
Sent: June 28

Ok, I'm laughing my head off after reading your email.

On the delicate note ... I've discussed this with a few friends. One friend continued her waxing regimen ... as I have never gone that route I didn't feel that now is an appropriate time to start.

I guess I do what I would consider "fly blind." Yes, I just grab a razor and hope for the best. I'm sure it's some weird obscure pattern—something resembling a crop circle—but my options are limited and times are desperate. I have another friend who had her husband help her out. This is not an option for me ... however it may work for others.

Yet another friend stood by the sink with a hand mirror, hair clippers, and a razor. I'm sure things are wild and unruly, and I hope that the medical staff can actually find the child through the forest.

Kim, I wish you luck ... you may want to have the phone nearby to dial 911 just in case of extreme blood loss.

From: Kim
To: Natalie, Celeste
Sent: June 28

Here is the problem I forgot to mention ... if I actually use a razor, then I totally break out. Same thing with Nair. Therefore, I use an electric razor. I do plan to go to my wax lady for a basic bikini, but I am still worried about one or two being missed and growing ten inches long.

Ben said he would help out, but he wasn't going to any extremes ... more, let us say, "topical" as opposed to "in the trenches." So I do not feel he is a great option at this point. Besides, if I allow him in that close of proximity to me, he may get aroused and I'll be damned if I am willing to be intimate at this point in the game.

At least now I know I am not the only one concerned about this issue.

From: Celeste
To: Natalie, Kim
Sent: June 28

I am laughing so hard I cannot see.

I would have to agree with Natalie. My normal regimen during this time is to "fly blind." I did this with Anna and I am doing this again.

I have been thinking about this email all day and laughing. Honestly, there is nothing like honest, yet slightly crazy, girlfriends.

Delivering the Truth

Bikini waxing is safe but can be extremely painful even for the waxing veteran because of the increased sensitivity and blood flow in the nether regions. Nair is safe because the cream doesn't get absorbed into the bloodstream. Obviously, shaving (aka: flying blind) is safe but could potentially be unsafe depending upon your visibility.

July

From: Kim
To: Natalie, Celeste
Sent: July 1

I'm looking at maternity t-shirts online. There is one that is perfect for me …

"If you didn't put this baby in here then don't even think about touching my belly." I love it! Problem is … the fools made it with a normal t-shirt not a maternity one! WTH!

Delivering the Truth

What team are you on? Are you on the team that worships her inner goddess and embraces the glowing and blissfully pregnant belly? Or are you with us and on team Keep-Your-Hands-to-Yourself?

List of people who are not allowed to touch your pregnant belly:

- Random stranger
- Lecherous father-in-law
- Overzealous coworker
- Lady behind you in line at the grocery store checkout

From: Natalie
To: Kim, Celeste
Sent: July 4

Tell me it's perfectly normal to put stretch mark cream on my feet. I think the skin is going to fall off. I think I may be going barefoot to work tomorrow. Again, WTH?

Happy 4th of July. I have enjoyed my last days off as a DINKY [dual income, no kids—yet]. We got a lot of loot at my second shower on Saturday. We had a lot of duplicates (thanks to our baby registry getting screwed up), but my sister and I exchanged lots of stuff and now we are as prepared as we are going to be. Bring on the contractions!

I start my fun exams with my doctor on Friday. I'm sure I'm 5 cm dilated and ready to deliver ... HAHAHAHAHAHAHAHA.

How are you feeling? How was your 4th?

 From: Kim
To: Natalie, Celeste
Sent: July 6

So, Nat, anything better with the midnight puking episodes? Anything I should know about the last month of pregnancy? Are you getting excited or anxious?

From: Natalie
To: Kim, Celeste
Sent: July 6

The midnight puking has subsided ... and is just replaced with unending heartburn. I'm so uncomfortable I think I could lie down and cry. I can only cram my feet into my tennis shoes. I can't feel my right hand and I'm just achy. I'm officially 36 2/7 weeks. I see my OB tomorrow and he'll check me. I'm really hoping that this kiddo comes early.

His movements are no longer gentle—they are jabbing kicks that hurt. Some poor soul was nice enough to tell me that she thinks I've dropped. I'm sure she was just humoring me.

I'll let you know what my doctor says tomorrow. Since it's an invasive exam I guess I'll have to "fly blind" tomorrow morning and try to clean things up in the nether region—wish me luck.

We are officially ready to bring him home. I'm going to clean and reorganize this weekend and then I'm going to sit in the empty bathtub and pray to all things holy that my water breaks.

How are you guys feeling?

Dr. Bob says

Most everyone is aware that nausea and vomiting in pregnancy is not only common, but normal. This most typically is understood to be in the first half of the pregnancy. However, it can be normal, although much less common, in the third trimester to have recurrences.

Again, as a male, I have not had the pleasurable experience; however, I was given a great description by my saintly wife who said it is like having a chronic hangover ... that I understood.

If a later pregnancy recurrence of vomiting happens, be sure to let your health care provider know to make sure it is not something more concerning. However, if felt to be normal, often times smaller and more frequent meals (grazing) can be helpful.

This often goes hand-in-hand with heartburn or reflux (gastroesophageal reflux disorder called GERD). Avoid caffeine and chocolate ... decide if pleasure is worth the pain. Antacids are fine. Discuss this with your health care provider. Avoid reclining immediately after eating ... and good luck.

From: Kim
To: Natalie, Celeste
Sent: July 6

I have had the worst heartburn for several weeks now. I keep my Tums by my side at all times. I also take fish oil pills two to three times a day, which really helps. Of course, I burp fish but I would rather do that than have a searing pain tearing up and down my throat.

My brother's girlfriend (who is a nurse) was kind enough to tell me that my feet are starting to swell. Really!? I usually wake up with a backache since I cannot sleep in a comfortable position. I really need to make an appointment for a massage and quit talking about it!

Interesting about his movements actually starting to hurt. There have been a few times where she goes so low that I feel like she is trying to push her way out above my pubic bone. She hasn't done that since last week so I can't complain. I am twenty-eight weeks as of the 4th of July. Everyone keeps asking if time has gone by really fast. I think it is dragging on and on and on.

All my baby showers are getting planned, and I am taking my best friend with me to register this weekend. I told her I didn't want to register for a bunch of things I didn't need and since she has three under three I figured she would know best. No point in taking Ben with me unless it is electronic.

I bet it was fun getting everything together and organized. I wish my stepson's bunk bed would get here so we can set that up and start getting the room ready. All of her furniture is down in the basement.

On another sad note, my belly button has begun to pop out. I asked Ben if he could see any stretch marks yet. He looked at one side and said, "No" and then the other side and said, "Yes." I almost had a heart attack then and there but then he said, "Oh, wait, that is just a line from your pants." When did you get your first stretch mark?

I too will be glad when this venture is over and I'm banking on the fact that I will be overjoyed with the results.

Dr. Bob says

It is very common for belly buttons to go from an "inny" to an "outie" in pregnancy. This typically occurs when the turkey is done! Actually it typically occurs later in the pregnancy, however, with subsequent pregnancies it can occur earlier. It will return to normal after the delivery. If you have concerns, simply ask your health care provider.

From: Natalie
To: Kim, Celeste
Sent: July 6

Tums have become my nighttime friend as well. They live on my nightstand. Last night I left the bottle in the bathroom, and I just suffered through the night because I could not tolerate getting out of bed to get them.

That is so helpful of your brother's girlfriend to point out the swelling. Our friends, over the 4th of July, were nice enough to point and laugh at my feet and cankles. Then, when I covered them up with a towel so I wouldn't offend anyone with their horrible appearance, they felt sorry for me. JERKS ... as if this is a good time for me.

I think I'm going to try and do the massage and pedicure this weekend. I'll see if I can get it. I can't afford it but I don't care.

Time has gone fast up to this point. Now it is dragging because I'm always running to the bathroom to check to see if I've lost my mucous plug (let me tell you how horrified I am to SEE that) or if I've lost any fluid besides the normal peeing of my pants. Yes, it's a glamorous time in my life.

As I think I've told you I've taken to wearing the grandma panties to hold the lovely pad (which I haven't worn this big of a pad since I was fourteen) in place.

Brad managed to touch the outline of the grandma pants one night and started to utter, "Hey ... what's going on here?"

I said in a very loud and angry voice, "Just say it, just get it all out in the open because I can't take the teasing for the last few weeks!"

He then said, "What are you talking about ... I wasn't saying anything."

Smart man. It's embarrassing enough that I have to put them on every day, let alone the sheer terror of someone else witnessing me in them.

Stretch marks—I really haven't seen any. My boss said she thought she didn't have any either and then she took a mirror and looked at the underside of her belly. I've done that too and don't see any. I'm sure I have them, but my skin is so pale that I haven't seen any. I'm sure they will be more noticeable after the baby is born and I am left with a huge flabby gut to admire.

I've used stretch mark cream every day on my belly, boobs, and now my feet. My skin has started getting really itchy at night, which tells me it's at its absolute limit. My belly button is still an "inny" ... but it is really tiny and distorted. I think it just spread out instead of popped out. Hey, at least I have one good thing happening.

I'm over it ... eviction notice served. Thirty days or less to vacate the premises.

Dr. Bob says

Stretch marks in pregnancy could be one of the biggest concerns of pregnant women and one of the least understood issues by physicians. Officially known as *striae gravidarum*, stretch marks are not harmful in any way other than the concerns cosmetically.

It is estimated that anywhere from 50 to 80 percent of pregnant women get stretch marks. They can occur outside of pregnancy as well: during puberty, weight gain, or even weight loss. They can appear not only on the belly, but also on the thighs, breasts, hips, and even buttocks.

Generally they start out pink, purple reddish brown, or dark brown depending on your skin color. They may initially have some itching with them due to the stretching of the middle layer of skin. Later, they fade to a white or silver. It is impossible to predict who will get stretch marks although there are risk factors such as increased weight gain, multiples, genetics (family history), adolescent moms, too much amniotic fluid, and hormonal changes later in pregnancy.

In spite of all the ads you see, there is no reliable evidence of any cream or special voodoo treatment to prevent stretch marks. Good hydration with lots of water and any moisturizing lotion is probably as good as any over-hyped product ... and cheaper.

The good news is that stretch marks usually become significantly less visible and noticeable after pregnancy. This will usually occur about six to twelve months after delivery. They do not totally go away; however, there is some evidence that certain dermatological treatments may help lighten the appearance even more (but not totally) while lightening your wallet significantly. You can talk to your dermatologist if you are interested.

From: Kim
To: Natalie, Celeste
Sent: July 6

Too funny. I guess I should clarify ... my belly button is stretching out as well ... no immediate pop out, just not really there anymore. I didn't think about the stretch marks being so faint you can't see them until after delivery and shrinkage.

On another note, I saw a friend last week who delivered her daughter three weeks ago, and she looks like she was never pregnant. I was amazed! I asked her how she did it and she claims not to know. This is even her third baby. She said this did not happen with her two boys. She has had a c-section with every one of them. I was totally thrilled to see her in that good of shape and am actually starting to believe it will happen to me as well.

I am horrified that I will be in my research methods class and my water will break. Let me ask you this: are you wearing a pad to "catch" the mucous plug in the event it comes down the hatch or simply for the occasional leakage?

From: Natalie
To: Kim, Celeste
Sent: July 6

I don't know about stretch marks. I find it hard to believe that I am lucky enough not to have any. I don't have any red lines. I do have some veins happening on my boobs and belly—but if I drink A TON of water they are less noticeable. So that gets me more motivated to chug water.

I have two friends who looked amazing immediately after delivering. Both were workout freaks before and during pregnancy, and both were breastfeeding models of society. My other friends all look great after delivering. Celeste, I'm including you in this group of tiny-waisted girls that you cannot tell delivered a baby.

Then there are those girls who carry around the extra weight forever. No one wants to be this girl.

I've read that 85 percent of women have regular strong contractions (meaning get to the hospital) before their water actually breaks ... so that is good news. As far as the pad, it is used to "catch" all kinds of fun and exciting things like discharge and urine. If a plug happens to land in there as well, it's just an added bonus.

Dr. Bob says

When the "bag of water" breaks before labor starts, this is called Premature Rupture of Membranes (PROM) when it occurs at term. Prior to term gestation (37 weeks EGA) it is called Preterm Premature Rupture of Membranes (PPROM). PROM occurs in 8 percent of pregnancies and is generally followed fairly quickly (within four to six hours) by the onset of labor. Half of women will deliver within five hours and 90 percent will go into spontaneous labor within twenty-four hours.

So the good news is that odds are only one out of twelve ladies will have their water break before labor starts. Most will have it occur in the hospital.

From: Kim
To: Natalie, Celeste
Sent: July 6

I am very dismayed to report that the stretch marks on my boobs (purple-ish looking lines) that had faded last month are back again. Furthermore, I think I am starting to leak a little bit as there is something on my bra at times when I take it off. I am pleased to report that several people have said I am the cutest pregnant person they have seen and others have been nice enough to remark, "You are seven months! You can barely tell you're pregnant." I have now included all those people in my will.

Dr. Bob says

Breast leakage known as galactorrhea (milk secretion from the nipple) results from the combination of effects of multiple hormones. This is not uncommon prior to delivery and can even occur in the first trimester. Typically it is pale and watery and there is nothing wrong and does not imply anything about milk production after delivery. As you can tell, pregnancy is a time of *many leaks* from *many places*. However, if you notice any blood fluid from the nipple, you should notify your health care provider.

From: Celeste
To: Natalie, Kim
Sent: July 6

Breast leakage is not too fun. I have already had this happen to me and am nowhere near delivery ... can't wait to start the breast pads again. Those are a joy and it is really fun when the leakage is so severe that your shirt is wet. Very glam.

And leakage down there is now starting to cause paranoia at my house. I am paranoid that I will go into preterm labor.

I have Braxton Hicks contractions at least five times a day and get freakish about making sure of the time they happen to ensure I don't have four within an hour. I should invest in a few pads as I am also getting freakish about any form of discharge and secretly think anything that comes out is amniotic fluid. I am constantly stopping the flow of urine every time I am in the bathroom to make sure I am not having a "gush" of fluid instead of pee. Of course to everyone else, I am "practicing my kegel exercises."

I really like the idea of stretch mark cream on the feet. We should market that.

I pray that you both have your babies at thirty-seven weeks. Me, I am shooting for October 18th. I am sure on October 14th I will be cursing myself for scheduling a c-section so damn late.

Dr. Bob says

Braxton Hicks contractions are sometimes called prelabor contractions. They were named after a British gynecologist—John Braxton Hicks—in 1872. Braxton Hicks contractions are generally felt to be of no consequence and more of an annoyance.

However, the difficult part is distinguishing Braxton Hicks contractions, or false labor, from the real thing.

Although there are certain aspects that describe one from another, pregnant women cannot for certain differentiate real ones from not. We can all tell you that we have seen ladies come in with complaints of "only Braxton Hicks contractions" who are well in preterm labor. On the other hand, we have seen ladies who come in swearing to the Lord they are going to deliver—NOW, and they go on for weeks or months before they deliver.

I usually tell patients if they have more than four contractions in an hour to get off their feet, empty their bladder, and drink fluids. If they persist with more than four an hour, call their health care provider regardless of whether they think they are Braxton Hicks or not.

From: Kim
To: Natalie, Celeste
Sent: July 6

First of all, I can't seem to get the kegel exercises down because I have no feeling in those muscles. Secondly, I hate to say this (no, not really), Celeste, you are totally paranoid. You are not going into preterm labor. This is your second time around ... you are supposed to be strong for us here!

Pray for me to go right up to my due date or beyond. The longer I go, the more school stuff I get done!

As for leakage, I am guessing I am going to be one of those women who imagines she hears a baby crying and leaks all over the place. As for the nether regions, I keep waiting for Ben to say something since he does the laundry, but I don't think he has noticed the minor changes in the overall cleanliness of my underwear so I am not going to draw his attention to it.

On another note, I was sitting in one of those fold-up chairs on the fourth of July and had my hands full of empty plates and I could not get out of it. This was a first for me and unfortunately my dad witnessed it and laughed so hard I seriously thought he was going to hyperventilate. Schmuck.

Dr. Bob says

Kegel exercises are pelvic floor exercises. The pelvic floor muscles are important in maintaining urinary control and keeping the pelvic organs in their proper place. During pregnancy the pelvic floor muscles can be stretched and weakened. This can result in problems controlling urine (think involuntary leaking here) and allowing pelvic organs to prolapsed or sag. If done correctly, kegel exercises can help prevent this from occurring. Kegels can be done during and after pregnancy safely ... even discreetly while you are sitting at a red light. [If you try to stop the flow of urine, you're using the muscles you want to strengthen.]

 From: Natalie
To: Celeste, Kim
Sent: July 6

Leakage from the upstairs region has not happened to me ... yet. I've got all the proper equipment and protection if it occurs.

The downstairs region is a bit more troublesome, which strikes fear in my heart for my internal exam with my doctor tomorrow. Gross!

From: Kim
To: Celeste, Natalie
Sent: July 6

Damn! I didn't even think of that! Well, at least the MD's are used to it. I am not prepared if I have a major gushage of the boobage.

From: Natalie
To: Kim, Celeste
Sent: July 7

I bit the bullet and scheduled a pedicure and one-hour massage at the salon tomorrow. Pedicure $50, Massage $60, lying on my stomach for an hour ... priceless!

Celeste, I hope they don't rub my butt. I've told you how much I can't stand that!

I figured if Brad can go out of town to play softball for seven weekends in a row, I can do something nice for myself. They told me to bring flip flops to wear out of the salon ... HA! My flip flops don't usually fit me anymore.

I'll let you know what I think.

Dr. Bob says

Pedicures in pregnancies, are they safe? They are safe. The concern that some have talked about is in reference to reflexology [an alternative medicine technique that applies pressure to specific points or zones on the feet to bring about physical change in the body]. There is no good reliable data that indicates reflexology either leads to term labor or preterm labor. If in fact it did, I would learn how and be the most popular guy around pregnant ladies. Then I could retire. So go ahead with the pedicures, but just be sure the tools are sterilized between uses to prevent the transmission of fungal infections to the feet. Yuck.

 From: Natalie
To: Kim, Celeste
Sent: July 7

This morning I got out of the shower and wrapped my towel around me. I went waltzing around the house getting my clothes ready and letting the dogs out. When I got back to the bathroom and looked in the mirror I noticed that my belly is so enormous that a HUGE gap is being left in the towel in a very strategic place. Yes, the belly makes the towel not fit around me.

Wonderful. Good thing I noticed before a neighbor or my husband did.

From: Celeste
To: Natalie, Kim
Sent: July 7

I invested in a size XL robe that was on super-duper clearance for this specific purpose. The open towel look usually isn't very attractive.

You have to let me know how the pedicure and massage go ... I have never been to the place you are going so I cannot guarantee they will not touch the butt. I have never had a massage where they touched the butt. Just tell the girl that you have issues with butt massage. She will probably laugh at you. It does feel good when they get the area right above your tailbone— right above the butt crack and below where normal jeans would sit (remember normal jeans with zippers and a button?).

I have been going to the chiropractor and he is my new best friend. I was having severe pain in the left hip and now it is gone. He is a miracle worker.

Let us know how the visit with your doctor goes ... and if he made you do the "frog-leg." You should stop by my house after your appointment ... just a few blocks away! I could serve you lemonade and you could be attacked by my dogs. ☺

From: Kim
To: Celeste, Natalie
Sent: July 7

Uhm ... WTH are you talking about with the frog-leg?

I could care less if my towel gaps.

A deep massage to the glutes can feel good—you both have issues.

I was able to still paint my toes today! And they looked good!

From: Natalie
To: Kim, Celeste
Sent: July 8

Frog legs ... instead of stirrups.

Yes, the glutes were rubbed and I nearly cried due to pain. I am not a massage girl. Plus, my massage lady was barefoot and she was missing her second toe and I kept looking at it through the hole in the table.

 From: Kim
To: Natalie, Celeste
Sent: July 8

WHAT! That would be distracting to me. I would sit there and wonder why she is missing a toe and I wouldn't be able to shut my brain off and relax. On another note, I love massages but some people can definitely work your muscles over, which can be painful. I always tell them "not too much pressure" and then if it is too weak I tell them to kick it up a notch.

I would prefer stirrups.

 From: Natalie
To: Kim, Celeste
Sent: July 8

My doctor got called out for a delivery right before my appointment so his nurse just did the GBS (group beta strep) test. She said she could check me but it would be invasive and unless I've been having more than four contractions an hour she wouldn't recommend it. My pressure was good, but she was concerned about the amount of swelling—or protein I'm retaining. She gave me the big spiel about hypertension and what to look for. I have to weigh myself every morning (oh joy), and if there is a 3 pound or more change, I need to come in or go to the hospital right away.

She wants me to monitor his movements closely. She said four to seven movements an hour (well this doesn't happen, so I'm freaking myself out until he moves). She said I had to go home and put my feet up and drink water like I'm a camel and then they'll see me again in a week.

I told the nurse that I didn't know if I was having contractions, and she said, "You are having one right now"—so that was cool—at least now I know what I'm looking for. And I do have several each day, but so far not four in an hour.

I came home and told Brad all of this—he didn't seem too concerned which pissed me off, and now he's in South Dakota playing ball. He goes to Minneapolis next weekend to play. My next MD appt isn't until the 18th (which is AFTER his MN trip). I'm just fat and grouchy.

I did the pedicure today. It was nice but I was totally self-conscious about my legs and cankles.

That's what I know for now. Maybe I'll deliver before the 18th and totally escape being checked by my doctor until I deliver.

How is everyone else doing?

Dr. Bob says

Kick counts or fetal movement counts are a method for evaluating that the baby is doing well in utero. There are many different ways to do kick counts/movement counts, and one is not necessarily better than another. The bottom line is that reassuring baby movements is a way to let us know babies are enjoying the intrauterine environment. Ask your doc how he or she likes to have them done—kick counts are a safe, noninvasive, cheap way of monitoring your baby ... do it!

From: Kim
To: Natalie, Celeste
Sent: July 9

I have to admit that I am a bit confused as well. My MD asked if I was having Braxton Hicks yet. How am I supposed to know? I occasionally feel tight below my belly button but that is about it. I would be freaking myself out about trying to count how many times I felt the baby move in an hour.

From: Celeste
To: Kim, Natalie
Sent: July 10

The tightening below your belly is probably Braxton Hicks. Usually you can feel it wrap around to the sides too. Pay close attention the next time you feel that. See if it goes anywhere other than right below your belly button.

I am having about five Braxton Hicks each day, which surely means I am going into preterm labor.

What a crappy day outside. I guess today is better than this coming weekend ... 100 degrees. Do the weather gods not know we are pregnant and can't stand the heat?

So is Brad just trying to act unimpressed so that he doesn't freak you out more by worrying about your blood pressure? Maybe he is just trying to play it cool. But the nurse obviously did a good job freaking you out. Have they (doctor and nurse) not learned yet? Any seemingly small comment is going to send us over the edge—so the safest bet is to not say anything at all!

And four to seven times an hour for the baby to move? Let's say he has a really good workout and karate chops you for a minute, does that count as one movement or seven? And what about when he is napping? Wouldn't it be easier to just do "kick counts" twice or three times a day for an hour?

Maybe we should make a "gratitude" list ...

Things I am grateful for:

1. I can paint my toes.
2. I am not on bed rest.
3. The swelling has not reached my feet—just my fingers.
4. Maternity clothes still fit.
5. I can still sleep at night.

Feel free to add to the list as you are able.

From: Kim
To: Celeste, Natalie
Sent: July 10

My gratitude list ...

1. That I can complain about everything with the pregnancy because I was able to become pregnant and not have any serious complications (okay ... nor minor) so far.

2. That when I tell people I am seven months they look at me and say, "But you are so small!" (This felt good until I saw Celeste yesterday and now I hate her profusely because she looks five months.)

3. That I have two other gals that are due near my time and I can check in with them to make sure everything I am experiencing is normal.

4. That I can still paint my toenails as well.

5. That I got what I was hoping for with being pregnant with a girl!

I made an appt with my dermatologist. The leprosy (a.k.a. the acne) on my face is getting to be too much for me to handle. Ben has now started calling me, "My sweet little leper." If I wasn't able to laugh at myself this would not be so funny.

 From: Natalie
To: Kim, Celeste
Sent: July 10

This is a little difficult for me this morning because I am a grouch. Maybe this will help me shake the mood.

Things I'm grateful for ...

1. The ability to become pregnant and that my body has carried the pregnancy this far without complications.

2. I have a bathroom in my bedroom.

3. I have a new bottle of Tums on my nightstand.

4. I am not on bed rest.

5. I am wearing crocs today so my feet can swell as much as they want—they have plenty of room.

6. My husband still loves me. He joked with me last night about my cankles, which means he is feeling lucky—or at least he knows he can outrun me.

7. I have a sister who will give me breaks from child care any time I want.

8. I have two friends that are pregnant with me and I can voice my concerns about terrible possibilities that likely won't happen.

9. I have the means to support a child with lots of cool baby gear and family/friend support.

Okay, my back is breaking from sitting at the computer. Gotta go waddle off and do some work.

 From: Kim
To: Celeste, Natalie
Sent: July 10

Oh, whoa, my underwear ... I'm just going to blame this one on Natalie because I feel she jinxed me.

I have all my cotton bikini undies from Victoria's Secret. I usually buy a few new pairs every six months or so and throw out the ones that need replacing. Lately I've noticed that they are getting holes by the elastic band. "This is unusual," I say to myself but I move on with daily living and only think about it when they are coming off or going on.

Enter in last night when I got up to pee five times. I usually never sleep in my underwear because I prefer some type of loose pajama bottom instead, but they were in the wash so underwear it was. I realized that somehow my undies had shrunk! They used to fit. Had Ben done something funky with the wash? Perhaps boiling them in hot water so they would shrink and weakening them so they would become holey?

Of course, I pull on a fresh pair today and I hear ... riiippppppppp!

I may have to buy larges instead of my mediums in case he shrinks more of my underwear.

Dr. Bob says

On the subject of ass expansion, I plead the Fifth Amendment ... please.

 From: Natalie
To: Kim, Celeste
Sent: July 10

I knew mine had shrunk when they left painful red marks on my hips. It must be something with our plumbing, or some strange chemical in the water that made them shrink. I went and bought larges too—much more comfortable—and I can either pack them away with the maternity clothes or throw them out.

Don't blame yourself, or Ben ... blame some weird random chemical in the water. That seems to make more sense.

From: Celeste
To: Kim, Natalie
Sent: July 10

I am sure the problem is Ben's technique in the laundry room. That happened to me also, only it was my technique in the laundry that caused the shrinkage. Same thing happened to my friend Jamie too ... damn washer and dryer.

Regardless of whose fault it is, welcome to stage 2 in maternity underwear. I have been wearing the large Victoria's Secret cotton undies this pregnancy (stage 2) and things have been working out well. Actually, the large VS undies carried me until delivery day with Anna—I wish you the same good fortune.

Unfortunately, I think Natalie has moved beyond this stage to stage 3 in maternity underwear ... a sad day for any woman.

From: Kim
To: Celeste, Natalie
Sent: July 10

I think it would be helpful to all of us if you did not hold out on some of the information you acquired during your first pregnancy. This is the first I have heard about the different stages of underwear. When I heard your comment I immediately had a flashback to my bra experience of, "Do you want one that fits you now or one that you can grow into?"

By the way, who is still wearing their normal bra and when does one actually go and buy maternity bras?

Did I tell you guys that I registered at Babies R Us (BRU) on Saturday? It took me three damn hours! I about died afterward. Actually, I about died beforehand when my friend, Lori, stood there and talked to me about all the different bottles there were. I blacked out after she showed me the different nipples and how I had to be careful since even the same brand does not have nipples that fit each bottle they make, etc. etc. etc.

From: Natalie
To: Celeste, Kim
Sent: July 10

I'm not at stage 3—I'm at stage 2. I'm just wearing size large bikini underwear ... instead of my normal underwear ... let's get this straight.

I pray we never reach stage 3.

From: Kim
To: Natalie, Celeste
Sent: July 10

Are you sure? I swear you said you were wearing the granny panties. It's okay if you are Natalie, because Celeste and I will understand.

From: Natalie
To: Kim, Celeste
Sent: July 10

I consider these granny panties—as they are much different than what I wear regularly. Do I have to show you guys next time? For real ... please believe me.

From: Celeste
To: Natalie, Kim
Sent: July 10

I think what she is saying is that she is no longer going commando or wearing thongs.

I am still wearing thongs but only about once a week ... the rest of the time it is stage 2 underwear.

BTW, my baby hasn't moved all day, so I'm drinking Diet Mountain Dew as we speak.

Anna hasn't been to day care since July 3rd. I am ready to ship her to China. Stay-at-home mothers are a special breed. I think this situation is comparable to cat and dog people. You are one or the other. And no matter what happens in my life, I will always be a dog person who can't stay home with kids 24/7.

As for holding back on info I gathered along the way with Anna, the last time (if you remember, Kim) that you asked me about a situation (hemorrhoids) and I tried to tell you the truth, you were very upset about the answer. It is like walking a fine line that I can only cross when I feel it may be safe. Disclosing the underwear trauma felt safe today.

When is it nap time? And is it wrong to have your kid watch TV all day when they are awake?

Dr. Bob says

In regard to drinking Diet Mountain Dew as a response to decreased fetal movement, often times during the day, movements are not perceived as well due to busy schedules, maternal activity, or baby sleep cycles. If this occurs, get off your feet and lie on your side and do a kick count. It is fine to drink cold water, juice, or even soda ... although water and juice are better for you. If you are diabetic, go with cold water.

From: Kim
To: Natalie, Celeste
Sent: July 10

Breast versus bottle? What are you ladies planning on? Are you breastfeeding? And if so, what bottles did you end up getting? Bags or no bags? How do I know what nipples to get?

From: Natalie
To: Kim, Celeste
Sent: July 10

I'll give it a try. I got the Avent bottles—not the ones with the bags. Most of my friends liked these bottles the best. One of my friends swears by the drop-ins. I don't know ... I guess we can always try something different if this doesn't work. I also didn't buy a breast pump. I guess I wanted to see if the girls work before I invest $200 to $300.

From: Celeste
To: Natalie, Kim
Sent: July 10

I breastfed for the first eight weeks (possibly the worst eight weeks of my life) and then used the Avent bottles. Anna loved them. I liked that they were easy to wash (fat bottles, so you can actually get your fingers in them), and I didn't have to continually go to the store to buy drop-in refills. One less thing to think about.

I will be using the Avent bottles again ... after I torture myself with the breastfeeding stage ... just need to go and buy new nipples for them and get them out of whichever random box they are in and wash them. Also, did I mention before the different stages of nipples for bottles? Make sure when you buy nipples for your bottles that they are newborn stage not stage four or you will choke your baby.

As for formula type, I used what they gave me at the hospital.

And bras. I am still wearing a normal bra. I would go and buy a breastfeeding bra (inexpensive one) a week or two before your due date. That way you have one. And if you like it, you can just send someone out to buy another one exactly like it if breastfeeding works for you. I would also suggest buying a breastfeeding bra that doesn't have underwire to wear to bed because if you are breastfeeding, you will be wearing a bra 24/7. You only get to take it off in the shower.

If you can't find one that doesn't have underwire, then buy a loose fitting and very stretchy bra to wear to bed that you can easily pull down or up without unlatching.

Also, buy a pair of PJ's that button down the front. Frankly, the belly is quite a disgusting sight after delivery and you won't want anyone who is visiting to see your belly if you feel comfortable enough to breastfeed with them there. If you don't like button-down shirts on PJ's, then buy something that has ties at the shoulder. The only breastfeeding jammies I have seen at the stores are VERY ugly.

You will LIVE in your PJ's for the first two weeks, so spend some money on at least one good pair. You are going to want something that looks decent to wear at the hospital ... who wants to wear that sexy hospital gown that a million other people have worn before you?

And I strongly suggest getting a robe to go along with you to the hospital ... if you have PJ bottoms, there is no hiding the gigantic pad between your legs ... so the robe does very well at this when you feel like taking a stroll outside your room. And you will need slippers too.

Anna is asleep. I think I deserve ice cream.

From: Kim
To: Natalie, Celeste
Sent: July 10

Good info about the bras, bathrobe, and pajamas. This is the kind of helpful information I am talking about!

I did buy the Avent bottles but my friend said that when you pump it is nice to put it in the little bags and throw them in the freezer as opposed to having a ton of bottles in your freezer. There is also a convenient little storage container for the bags, and you can write the date and time on the bags.

Then she said it is easier to thaw the bags by throwing them in a glass of hot water. So I think I got some of each because I registered for those bottles and the bags.

She has a Medela pump so I am borrowing hers and just bought the new accessories that went with it. I also registered for a hand pump for when I am at school because the girl who signed me up said she was in school and she bought a little travel one to use because she would get so uncomfortable. This was halfway into the Babies R Us visit so now you can see why I was immediately overwhelmed.

From: Celeste
To: Kim, Natalie
Sent: July 10

Pumping and freezing. I just got the breastfeeding freezer bags and froze them in that. Put it in a glass of hot water to thaw and pour the bag into the bottle ... It wasn't really that much of an ordeal.

I only have a handheld pump and it worked fine. Of course (this may be too much info so close your eyes if you aren't ready) there were times when I was without a pump and Anna wasn't hungry and I thought I might die. I resorted to manually expressing the milk in a bottle in order to restore sanity. Even more depressing is that I had to do this in front of John. He was nice enough to pretend like he didn't care.

From: Kim
To: Celeste, Natalie
Sent: July 10

I am laughing so hard I may leak! I am getting a mental image of you leaning over a bottle and squeezing your boobs! Now see, this is where my nasty husband would say, "Need help with that?"

Good to know that the freezer bags work well. I plan to breastfeed for six months (ask me again after two months though) so that is why I am using the electric one so I can bring it to work or wherever.

I need to go wipe the tears of laughter from my eyes now!

From: Natalie
To: Celeste, Kim
Sent: July 10

Holy crap ... I just broke my hip falling out of my chair from giant outbursts of laughter. Your husband needs some sort of award or monetary compensation. Wow.

Delivering the Truth

In hindsight, breastfeeding can be a successful experience for both mom and baby. To increase your chances of success we suggest reading up on the topic, going to a breastfeeding class before delivery, and learning about breastfeeding groups in your community. Also, most hospitals have very helpful lactation consultants who are willing to assist you at any stage of your pregnancy. It is extremely helpful if you have good friends or family members who have had success in this. They will have many tips and can provide guidance as needed. Research shows breast milk is the best for babies!

 From: Kim
To: Celeste, Natalie
Sent: July 10

Nosebleeds ... does anybody else get these? Normally, I wake up and after I blow my nose I see that I had been bleeding during the night (not enough to get on the pillow—only up in my nose).

Today I am typing and I feel some liquid drop out of my nose and I look down and it is blood (which also conveniently splattered on the handrest of the keyboard). Now, I have heard that doctors hate operating on red heads because we are "bleeders," but now I am paranoid that I am going to bleed out during delivery.

Dr. Bob says

Nosebleeds in pregnancy are both common and normal as long as they stop relatively easily. In pregnancy the blood volume increases and hormone levels change. This results in the nasal membranes becoming swollen and dry. The condition can lead to more frequent nosebleeds. These swollen membranes can also lead to nasal congestion.

A few things can help. A humidifier may help. Drink plenty of water, saline nasal spray, and petroleum jelly may help coat the nasal membranes. Cold dry weather may make the nosebleeds worse.

Although, I never argue with a Labor and Delivery nurse or my wife, there is little to no data to support the myth that redheads bleed more than other women. So, redheads, fear bleeding no more than your blonde or brunette counterparts.

From: Natalie
To: Kim, Celeste
Sent: July 10

I had bloody noses up until about my third trimester. My nose was always very dry. Same thing as you have going on. But now it's back to normal. Except, I snore LOUD! I've woken myself up twice—probably my body waking me up before I choke to death or have some major apnea episode. Brad doesn't even bother waking me up anymore. I hope that goes away after I drop this weight.

Good news. Today a nurse at work told me I look "ready to deliver," so tonight is the night, right?

Dr. Bob says

Three things I've never heard of a pregnant lady doing: burping, snoring, or farting ... or at least every pregnant woman thinks she is the only one. Welcome to manhood, ladies—common and normal.

Snoring in pregnancy is very common in pregnancy because of nasal congestion and weight gain. It is primarily an annoyance ... to your husband. Occasionally it can be associated with sleep apnea or gestational diabetes.

From: Natalie
To: Celeste, Kim
Sent: July 11

Last night I found trace amounts of blood on toilet paper. I consider this a good sign, right?

From: Kim
To: Natalie, Celeste
Sent: July 11

I'm gonna have to say I have no frickin' clue what this means since I haven't read past twenty-nine weeks in my "Your pregnancy week by week" book. I defer to Celeste.

From: Celeste
To: Natalie, Kim
Sent: July 11

I would think so, but I would ask one of the nurses for sure! Wouldn't that be exciting if it was the "start" of things happening!

From: Natalie
To: Kim, Celeste
Sent: July 11

I keep waiting for some telltale sign of labor ... none yet ... that I know of. When I say "trace amounts," I really mean it.

Brad is still going to Minnesota this weekend and he keeps asking me if I think he should go? I DON'T KNOW! I would hate for him to stay and have nothing happen but what if something happens and he has to rush back. Boys are dumb ... of course he shouldn't go!

Dr. Bob says

EDC = estimated date of confinement = in other words, your due date. Naegele's rule estimates the EDC. Start with the first day of LMP (last menstrual period) add 1 year, subtract 3 months and add 7 days. The answer is your due date. This was established in 1830 and assumes a regular 28-day cycle. Pregnancies are measured as 40 weeks from first day of the LMP. Pregnancies today are typically dated by a known certain LMP confirmed by ultrasound, or by ultrasound. Approximately only 4 percent of babies are born on their due dates.

From: Kim
To: Celeste, Natalie
Sent: July 11

When we say "the start" of things happening, could this mean within a week OR does this mean it could still be another three weeks before she goes into labor? My office is like a sauna today—just thought I would share.

From: Natalie
To: Kim, Celeste
Sent: July 11

I think it means I could still have three to five weeks left ... but there is light at the end of the tunnel. The last possible day would be August 12th—being ten days late.

From: Kim
To: Natalie, Celeste
Sent: July 11

I know I have no idea what I am talking about here (since I am not totally uncomfortable yet), but the later I go, the more I can get done with school/practicum.

I remember my friend telling me her husband thought that he could still go watch the Huskers last year at the bowl game since the baby was due the week after. She had to have the doctor tell him that the due date is actually a guestimate and he should not go out of town anytime around that date. Men ...

From: Natalie
To: Kim, Celeste
Sent: July 11

Yeah, if I had stuff to do I'd be okay with going late—but I don't.

Yes, men are dense ... what do you do?

Delivering the Truth

This piece of advice is for the partner of the preggo: Since your partner's life has been put on hold for the last nine months (or longer!), your life can also go on hold. We are sorry if there is a big bowl game, a men's stag party in Vegas, or it's hunting season, parenthood starts before the baby is born.

From: Celeste
To: Natalie, Kim
Sent: July 11

The general rule is that if Brad leaves, you will go into labor. If he doesn't, you won't. Law of nature.

I had a very strange dream last night/this morning. I was meeting someone (a friend?) and we needed to stop by a television "set" of a reality show they were on. I got stuck being on the "adventure" show for one episode. So I am in this car (I have no idea who was driving) with a bunch of people who were on the reality show along with Anna. We were talking about how we hoped it wasn't going to be a long "adventure" because we had Anna with us and it was getting late at night.

Then all of a sudden, the car plummets off the side of a cliff and is heading toward water—like the ocean or a lake or something—and all I can think about was how pissed I was that they would do this to me when I never signed a contract with the TV show and I was pregnant and that Anna was in the car. It was a convertible with the top open and we all came out of the car (no seatbelts?), and I saw Anna falling faster than I was, so I grabbed her and held her close to me and then I woke up.

What do you think?

From: Natalie
To: Celeste, Kim
Sent: July 11

Oh jeez ... you are crazy. That is what that dream means. Sorry to tell you. You've got it bad.

I will just plan on going into labor this weekend. I'll pencil it in.

From: Kim
To: Celeste, Natalie
Sent: July 11

I don't know what to make of the dream. Weird. On the dream note, after I had asked you about what hiccups felt like, I had a dream that I went to the doctor ... you were with me ... and they told me the baby had died and I kept saying ... but she was just hiccupping! That one was not fun.

It is confirmed. I am having Braxton Hicks. I have them usually when I do stairs. Must start monitoring that more closely.

From: Natalie
To: Celeste, Kim
Sent: July 12

Last night I woke up abruptly at 4:30 a.m. with pretty intense back pain and menstrual cramp pain. I got up and started walking around. I had about four pains every fifteen minutes or so. But when I laid back down at about 5:30, they went away. Again, no bleeding or loss of fluid. Do you think these are contractions? I'll ask the RNs down on the Labor and Delivery unit for sure ...

No matter what, I packed my suitcase this morning (except all my daily use stuff) just in case. Maybe I'm just psyching myself out since Brad will be leaving.

Celeste, did you have contractions before your c-section with Anna?

 From: Kim
To: Natalie, Celeste
Sent: July 12

It sounds like contractions to me. My doctor said yesterday that if I had intense back pain along with abdominal cramping and it happened four times in one hour I needed to call. At least ... I think that is what she said. It all makes sense at the time she says it and then a day later I find myself saying ... was it intense pain in my foot or my back and was it four times in an hour or sixty-two?

From: Natalie
To: Kim, Celeste
Sent: July 12

The nurses said it sounds like contractions but it pooped out. They said if it would have continued to get closer together I should have at least called or come in. Since I have to work anyway ... I figured I'm safe around these parts. So far ... no more contractions.

I never remember what my MD or RN says at my appointments either. Last time they gave me the big spiel on PIH (pregnancy-induced hypertension) and I can barely remember it—give me a pamphlet, people!

From: Kim
To: Natalie, Celeste
Sent: July 12

Well, on the positive side, now you know what contractions feel like! No questions about it next time. It will be interesting to see if you have them again tonight or tomorrow. I'm guessing if you don't have any in those two days it might be safe for Brad to still go to Minnesota. Of course, remember what Celeste said about the law of averages!

Dr. Bob says

Preterm labor symptoms can be subtle and essentially the same as normal discomforts of pregnancy. That's what makes it difficult to clearly and easily differentiate preterm labor from normal everyday pregnancy complaints. The symptoms of preterm labor should always be discussed with your health care provider.

We typically tell patients if they have five or more contractions in an hour to empty their bladder, drink fluids, and lie down on their sides. If the contractions persist at greater than or equal to five in an hour after doing this, call your provider!

 From: Celeste
To: Kim, Natalie
Sent: July 12

On the negative side, does this mean you are going to have back labor? If so, that means you are going to want to get that epidural sooner rather than later! I never had contractions ... that I remember feeling anyway.

Remember when I was in the car accident and everyone (except me) flipped out? Well, I was apparently having contractions then (which is why I got yelled at and put on modified bed rest). I never felt them. And, when I was hospitalized for the actual delivery, I saw contractions registering on the strip, but never felt them.

Since you are going into labor soon, I need to know how I will be notified. It completely freaks me out that nobody is going to tell me you had the baby until I start questioning why you haven't sent an email in three days.

This question goes for Kim too.

From: Natalie
To: Kim, Celeste
Sent: July 12

I was fearing the back labor also. I think that may have been a clue. No more contractions to this point. I was going to send a big text message out after delivery ... then I can call or you can call.

Dr. Bob says

The term *back labor* is used to describe when the pain of labor is primarily felt in the lower back. It does really occur. It is sometimes felt that back labor occurs because of the position of the baby; however, this is not always the case. There is no way to prevent back labor, but there are ways to try and treat it. Some ways include physical activity (a walk), positional changes, massage, or medication.

From: Kim
To: Celeste, Natalie
Sent: July 13

I have to share my extremely good news. I was so sick and tired of having sleepless nights. Normally, I would wake up anywhere from one to four times just to go to the bathroom, but I would wake up in between those times to Ben's unique sleeping noises.

He brought home some earplugs. I thought I could never sleep with ear plugs in my ears but I tried them on Monday. I woke up once to pee. I wore them on Tuesday and only woke up once. I wore them last night and woke up at 5 a.m. to pee. I never woke up to his noises! I feel so rested to have three nights of sleep in a row! GOD BLESS EAR PLUGS! I want to kiss the inventor!

On another note, I had a massage last night by a student at the massage school. What a pathetic experience. I could barely feel him touching me. That is saying a lot since normally I am telling them, "Not so hard!" It was ridiculous! Plus, I thought the bed did not have any cutouts for my boobs because only the stomach was out. I didn't notice until the end that they did have cutouts! I was mad. My poor girls were squished for almost an hour! This is the first bad massage I had there. Grrr.

From: Natalie
To: Kim, Celeste
Sent: July 13

Earplugs are great. I gave Brad a pair but he never wears them. My massage table didn't have the boob cutouts either ...
You should try the salon by my house, although I think it was like $60 for an hour. I certainly felt the pressure ... I think I have a coupon for $5 off.

From: Kim
To: Natalie, Celeste
Sent: July 13

I might do that but I definitely want the boob cutouts next time. These gals are just too large to lie on like that. I have to say

I did feel lightheaded and a bit weird in my abdomen after lying on my stomach for that long. Did you?

From: Natalie
To: Celeste, Kim
Sent: July 13

Yeah ... I felt weird. My eyes had a hard time focusing (although I could have been blinded from seeing the therapist's missing toe) and my face felt really swollen. I think your blood just all settles in your belly. That is why you feel weird.

From: Celeste
To: Natalie, Kim
Sent: July 14

My newest paranoia: I have now had numerous people tell me how small I am ... which I have now turned into intrauterine growth restriction.

And good luck going into labor this weekend, Natalie!

From: Kim
To: Celeste, Natalie
Sent: July 14

Yes, I have already said I don't like you anymore for just that reason. However, a girl in class today asked me if I was sure I was almost thirty weeks because I sure didn't look it and seemed rather small. Usually I say, "Thanks!" but this really didn't come across like a compliment.

From: Natalie
To: Celeste, Kim
Sent: July 14

Brad is officially on the road and I have a wedding tonight so ... let the labor commence.

I did wake up last night with terrible back and groin pain again. I could barely heft myself out of bed. My poor body. Please get a sign for me that says "WIDE LOAD" ... this will make my life easier.

Have a good weekend, girls!

From: Natalie
To: Celeste
Sent: July 17

I just found out that our doctor will be out of town July 24th through August 7th. So unless I deliver in the next five days I'll get one of his coworkers. I'm kinda miffed.

From: Celeste
To: Natalie
Sent: July 17

I called to make my appt with our doctor today and heard that news ... I thought about you ... I would be pissed too. Ask him if he will induce you so he can deliver the kid. He just might say yes. He told me he would deliver me early and then let me fly to Oregon for my work's fiftieth-year celebration with a fresh scar and a newborn. Of course, I didn't take him up on that ...

But I would say something to him about all of the stress with the abnormal quad screen and that you wouldn't really want anyone other than him to deliver and since he will be gone for so long, couldn't he deliver you early ... and you have protein in your urine, so might as well deliver ...

Honestly, it never hurts to ask. The worst he could say is "no" and cuz he likes you, he just might say "yes."

From: Natalie
To: Celeste
Sent: July 17

I guess we'll talk about the induction/noninduction tomorrow. If I'm not dilated at all I'm not going to push it, but if things are happening then I might. I just don't want to be induced and go into labor and then end up with a c-section anyway.

What the hell is he thinking?

Brad was pushing really hard on my stomach last night. He likes to harass the kid to get a huge kick, but I kept thinking maybe it will piss the kid off enough to head for the exit. Either that or get a placental abruption and have a rush delivery. So far no luck. I'm weak ... I may go for the induction if offered.

Dr. Bob says

Induction is a medical procedure that is used to stimulate contraction resulting in cervical change and, we hope, a vaginal birth. This is done prior to labor starting on its own.

There are many reasons for inductions of labor. Generally they are undertaken when there is a risk associated with continuing the pregnancy. Elective inductions should not be done prior to thirty-nine weeks. And this perinatologist feels elective inductions should not be done in first-time moms due to the associated increased risk for cesarean sections if the induction fails. This is a very complicated discussion and deserves much more discussion than can be given here. If you have questions, discuss them with your health care provider.

From: Natalie
To: Kim, Celeste
Sent: July 18

Dilation Station
Come on cervix here we go
Let's get dilated and start the show
If you can't do it on your own
I'll be induced and more prone
For a—spell it girls—C—————S—E—C—T—I—O—N
Thought you cheerleaders out there would appreciate that.
Okay, off to jump down some stairs.

From: Natalie
To: Celeste, Kim
Sent: July 18

I have started feeling like crap, I ate and I feel worse. My back and lower stomach are hurting. It doesn't come and go though. It's constant. I tried to get into the MD early but he's booked ... so I'm still going at 4:15.

I want to lie down. I also feel like I'm going to spew from one end or the other (TMI ... TMI ... I know).

If this is labor, I don't like it.

From: Natalie
To: Kim, Celeste
Sent: July 19

I called Celeste last night, so she has already heard this part ... My appt. I was dilated 3 cm, 60 percent effaced and at a +2, so my doctor seemed to think "any day." The dilation was obviously due to the cheer. He asked if I had been having a lot of contractions. I told him I wasn't sure. I've been having cramping since the night before. He said those are contractions.

Yippie!

So I got home and was very excited to tell Brad (of course I had to explain what all these numbers meant). At about 6 p.m. I started timing my contractions. They were about every twenty minutes apart—sometimes they were eleven minutes—sometimes they were forty minutes.

But after about 10 p.m. I decided I was going to go to bed. Certainly I would wake up if something major was happening. I could not get comfortable so I got about two hours of sleep, but the contractions had pretty much quit or become very few and far between.

This morning I wake up and lost the good ole mucous plug. Let me tell you girls ... nothing can prepare you for that. NOTHING. I almost gagged. This next part is way TMI and WAY GROSS so ... skip it if you can't handle it.

Ready ...

It was like a big, huge, sneeze in your shorts

EWWWWWWWWWWWWWWWWWWWWWWWW!!!!

So, I work 10 to 6:30 today. I hope my water will break or something spectacular like that ... but I am definitely more uncomfortable today. More waddling and less walking like a normal person, so I'm carefully optimistic that he is on his way.

YAHOO!

I'll keep you posted ... of course.

 From: Kim
To: Natalie, Celeste
Sent: July 19

How exciting! I appreciate the forewarning on what to expect with the mucous plug. I found the description highly amusing as well! Hopefully your water will break while you are at work so you can just skip on down to L&D. What did Brad have to say? Did he turn slightly green?

From: Natalie
To: Kim, Celeste
Sent: July 19

No water breaking as of today.

Brad was horrified ... but then began asking me all these questions about it ... and I answered each one with the preface, "Do you really want to know this?"

He thinks it will be any day too ... please, please, please let that be true. He went to the grocery store today to stock up on easy food and food for company.

From: Celeste
To: Natalie, Kim
Sent: July 19

Well, better luck tomorrow ... Maybe you will sleep well tonight and then go into labor when you are well rested. ☺

As for me, I have worn my ass out today. I don't know if it is the heat or just doing too much today but I could have gone to bed at 7:15. I even declined Cold Stone Creamery tonight so I could go to bed ... it's a sad day.

From: Kim
To: Celeste, Natalie
Sent: July 20

I had not thought about stocking up on food/drinks for visitors. Damn! One more thing to do! Keep us posted on the happenings of today.

Delivering the Truth

Perhaps Natalie is more gracious than Kim and Celeste who felt it was totally acceptable to feed guests tap water and stale crackers. Do not feel obligated to feed your guests Martha Stewart–worthy hors d'oeuvres or a seven-course meal. Surely there is a Taco Bell down the street they can hit on their way home.

From: Celeste
To: Kim, Natalie
Sent: July 20

Well, I emailed Nat first thing this morning and asked if she was at work ... and it is now 1 hour and 45 minutes later, and she hasn't emailed back.

From: Natalie
To: Celeste, Kim
Sent: July 20

I'm here. I had an employee-of-the-month party to attend ... no water breaking ... not even a contraction since last night. Brad told me that now he thinks it's going to be an August baby. Damn him.

From: Celeste
To: Natalie, Kim
Sent: July 20

Oh that sucks. I was so hoping that you were admitted! Keep walking and standing as much as possible ... there has got to be something to the "gravity" thing.

From: Natalie
To: Kim, Celeste
Sent: July 20

I was hoping the same thing ... no luck.

I am trying to get all my desk work done so I can head down (HINT, HINT SUBLIMINAL MESSAGE HERE) to Labor and Delivery ...

I carried a bunch of heavy stuff down the stairs yesterday and even laid down on the floor a few times and got back up (very hard these days). I'm trying. I told Brad ... what if I get really dilated and don't have contractions ... then what. How far do they let you get dilated before they admit you and try to get things moving?

From: Kim
To: Natalie, Celeste
Sent: July 20

I didn't want to say too much but I was recalling friends of mine that walked around for days (well, okay, weeks) dilated to a certain number. Although I am SURE that will not be you since of course your water will break in the bathroom on the Labor and Delivery unit between seeing patients. Any more nastiness with the mucous plug or was that it?

 From: Natalie
To: Kim, Celeste
Sent: July 20

I guess I've surrendered the "any moment" idea of going into labor and have settled back into the next two weeks theory ... if it goes beyond that, I will have angry feelings.

Nothing as nasty as compared to yesterday morning ... but a lovely, yet small amount of discharge has continued.

 From: Natalie
To: Kim, Celeste
Sent: July 20

Talk about pouring salt into the wound. I just saw my doctor down on the floor at work and he said, "I really thought you'd be at least admitted by now."

Gee ... thanks.

I kicked him in the nuts.

From: Kim
To: Natalie, Celeste
Sent: July 20

But isn't it nice to hear the MD say that? Kind of gives you hope that it won't be two more weeks! I hope you didn't kick him too hard. He needs to be in prime condition to deliver your son. Plus, you don't want any type of retaliatory attacks during your delivery or thereafter (such as withholding pain meds!).

From: Celeste
To: Kim, Natalie
Sent: July 20

Or you could have said, "Then why don't you go ahead and admit me and start this thing before you leave the country!"

On a negative note, I have now resorted to bribing Anna with ice cream if she stays in bed for naptime instead of getting out and finding me every three minutes after I put her in her room ... I am a horrible excuse for a social worker and mother.

From: Natalie
To: Kim, Celeste
Sent: July 20

Well, he (my doc) is quick. He said that to me and headed for the door.

I think it's fine that you bribe your daughter with ice cream—it's for a good cause.

From: Kim
To: Celeste, Natalie
Sent: July 20

Your doctor is leaving the country? Or were you just kidding? Hell, yes, you better have the baby before he leaves. What nerve of him!

On another note, ice cream? Doesn't sound too bad to me. If it is given to her after she wakes up then it kind of sounds like *The Sleep Fairy* book. ☺ Hope you feel better now.

 From: Celeste
To: Kim, Natalie
Sent: July 20

Yes, our doctor is leaving for Germany on July 22nd ... and he will be gone until August 8th or some ridiculous date.

What is *The Sleep Fairy* book?

Yes. Ice cream after nap. That is her new thing—getting up a hundred times when you put her to bed. I am wondering if this is related to the move. Until a week ago, she has been the poster child for naptime and bedtime and sleeping twelve hours at night. And now she is horrible. She gets up a hundred times before she falls asleep. She woke up in the middle of the night last night and didn't fall back asleep for another hour until John laid in her bed with her (we won't let her sleep in our bed, so we will "sleep" in her bed at last resort).

I don't know what else to do. I am afraid that it is the move and this is a transitional period, but if it is, then I am afraid to change daycare facilities right now and then, if I wait to change daycare facilities until she is "settled," then who knows when that will be and then I will be having a baby. Am I over thinking this or stressing about nothing?

From: Kim
To: Celeste, Natalie
Sent: July 20

The Sleep Fairy book talks about just this issue—kids getting up constantly or in the middle of the night. In the beginning part it tells parents how to use the book and different things they should be aware of and then it is a pretty picture book to read to a child about the wonderful Sleep Fairy who will visit them when they are sleeping and leave them a gift ... but she will only leave them a gift if they sleep through the night and stay in bed. Seems to work pretty well.

That would suck that your doctor would not be there to deliver you, especially since you guys have such a personal relationship with him. I hope you will deliver before Saturday, Nat!

From: Natalie
To: Kim, Celeste
Sent: July 21

Still here ... 'nuff said.

From: Celeste
To: Natalie, Kim
Sent: July 21

My ass. I swear it is expanding by inches on a daily basis. I think it all happens while I sleep. I wake up in the morning and when I get dressed, my clothes don't fit near as well as they did the day before. My shirts are basically fine. It is the pants ... my ass, hips, and thighs.

My problem is that I LOVE sweets: ice cream, M&M's (which I normally hate) and basically any type of chocolate I can get my hands on. I am no longer a "kind of cute" pregnant girl. I am now the girl that people say, "Wow, she really expanded in all the wrong places during her pregnancy!"

And then John had the nerve to say to me, "Good thing you didn't watch Jay Leno the other night (or Dave, I can't remember which) cuz Heidi Klum was on and she is pregnant and looks awesome."

Whatever, buddy—pass the chocolate chip cookie.

 From: Kim
To: Celeste, Natalie
Sent: July 22

You could chop John up into little pieces for a comment like that and you would never get in trouble for it. Heidi Klum probably has a personal chef, yoga/pilates instructor and not near the stress that we have. Skinny Bitch. ☺ Besides ... I see you once a week and know for a fact that you still are quite small (it has been hard maintaining our friendship due to this fact) so you are obviously having retinal problems again.

Yes, my hips/thighs/ass have expanded as well. I broke down and bought bikini maternity underwear at Old Navy today ... of course, I did not buy the next size up because these are maternity underwear and they wouldn't dare make you wear a size bigger then you normally wear.

I hate to break it to you, Natalie, but you are going to have to hold off on delivering until after next Friday because I have a final and a research paper due this week and it will be too hard for me to get up to the hospital and visit you. Just letting you know in advance.

From: Natalie
To: Celeste, Kim
Sent: July 22

Your ass is not expanding. I just saw you last week. It's pregnancy-induced insanity that is making you think so. I have tree trunks for legs and waddle for God's sake. I don't want to leave the house.

As for John, he's either feeling lucky or brave to make a comment like that. Not nice. Brad likes to make silly, not nice comments to me and then run because he knows I cannot catch him. Heidi Klum hasn't eaten solid food since she was ten.

As for me not going into labor until next week, that seems to be fine. There is nothing going on with me physically. This is the time I hate being a procrastinator. Obviously I have passed that gene on and this kid is quite content until he has to be forced out. He'll probably live in our basement until he's thirty-five also. I have another appointment on Monday and I'm going to ask her to strip my membranes. I hear it hurts but I don't care. Pain now. Pain later. What's the difference?

In the meantime I've diagnosed myself with either dissociative disorder or at least poor bonding. I don't think I've bonded with this child. Everything I've read says this is normal and many moms don't bond with their children until they have delivered. I don't wish harm on him or anything like that. I just kind of feel like I have an extra appendage. Is that weird? Of course ... as I'm typing this I'm having a contraction.

I'm very grouchy these days also. How hot am I? A grouchy, swollen, fat lady with tree trunks for legs. I understand why in biblical times pregnant women were sent away from the other villagers and were not allowed to return until they restarted their periods. It just makes good sense.

 From: Kim
To: Celeste, Natalie
Sent: July 22

I recall that Celeste felt the same way when she was pregnant with Anna, and I have to admit that I too feel that way. I'm giving myself a week or two after delivery to actually feel a little more attached. Don't want to push myself too hard.

Speaking of pushing too hard (this is a TMI moment for you girls), I had the most horrible bathroom experience today and truly felt that if labor is half of what I felt on the toilet today then I am in big, BIG trouble.

Let me explain further. I was a normal twice-a-day-bowel-movement kind of gal before this whole pregnancy thing. Never a constipated day in my life. This morning I was assuming that (1) I would have to somehow give myself an enema or (2) I would need to go to the hospital for poo assistance. I am ever so fearful that I will obtain a hemorrhoid (horror of my horrors).

Of course, I was reading my stupid pregnancy book to see if they had any enlightening suggestions (which the damn fools did not) except to say, "Don't strain too hard because you could cause hemorrhoids." Well THANK YOU FOR THAT CRAPPY INFORMATION! I swear to the poo gods I will eat my bran cereal every day along with roughage. Amen.

Speaking of stupid husbands, I have always said how wonderful and supportive mine is. Telling me almost daily how adorable I am pregnant. However, last night we had our "date night" in the Old Market. To keep a very long story short regarding a parking spot that was totally ours and some f******* b**** in a BMW stole it from us, he totally humiliated me.

To keep this story even shorter, it involved me politely going to her window and tap tap tapping on it with a smile and him screaming profanity at her while hanging out the car window. I was so shocked and appalled that he would resort to this kind of behavior that I walked away.

Now, suffice to say that whenever I exert myself (which means, when I walk faster than a quick turtle or walk upstairs) I get Braxton Hicks. The man almost put me into labor on the cobblestones of the Old Market he made me so upset! I am not kidding I must have had five in one hour. To make matters worse, my feet swelled up to circus balloon size, which they have never done before so I was sure that he had upset both to the point where we would need to be hospitalized.

He smartly hurried to find another parking spot and found me ASAP and started the conversation with, "Before you even say anything, I am so sorry and I honestly feel sick to my stomach for what I did and I cannot believe I did that." I made him suffer for a while with tears, etc.

Dr. Bob says

Hemorrhoids in pregnancy are common. They are actually a form of varicose veins in the rectal area. They are often itchy and painful and can result in bright red bleeding that can cause great concern due to the difficulty for a woman to tell if the blood is vaginal or rectal. They occur more commonly when ladies get constipated.

Other risk factors are excessive weight, straining during bowel movements, and the pressure of sitting or standing for prolonged periods of time. Some things can help such as drinking lots of water and some juice (prune juice, yum), high fiber foods, and exercise unless your doctor has told you not to. Avoid excessive weight gain, go when you have to go, and avoid any long periods of sitting or standing.

If you are one of the lucky ones, there are many symptomatic treatments available, so talk with your health care provider. And remember, most hemorrhoids go away on their own.

Constipation is also a common problem for many pregnant women. It can be a difficult and painful problem in pregnancy. Although there are treatments, it is better to prevent the dam than to have to break it.

It can often be prevented by lifestyle choices. Drink lots of water. Also, prune juice works well in pregnancy. Try a glass a day and then experiment until the prune juice intake results in normal bowel habits.

Physical activity on a daily basis can help prevent constipation (even daily walks) by stimulating the digestive system. Also, increase your fiber intake.

Remember that iron will increase the likelihood of constipation. So if you are on iron, and most are, be diligent about the preventive recommendations.

If you still end up backed up, talk to your health care provider about softeners and laxatives. They can be used safely but discuss this before you make a trip to Walgreens.

From: Celeste
To: Kim, Natalie
Sent: July 23

I don't think I bonded with Anna until she was just shy of her second birthday. That instant love feeling that people talk about—that they have never loved anyone or anything more in their entire lives—didn't happen to me for a looong time.

I think that is why I don't like the infant stage. I resented this little baby for always needing me when all I needed was some time to myself, a little shuteye, and to eat a hot meal. She didn't allow me to do any of those things.

This is also why I think I hated breastfeeding so much. I didn't pump (except for the rare manual pumping moment), and I was literally the ONLY person that could feed her every two to three hours. Have you ever tried to do anything every two to three hours for thirty minutes at a crack and be functioning while doing it? It isn't possible.

So, don't worry about bonding ... that will happen one day when you least expect it. Until that day, just focus on doing what you need to do to get through the day with the least amount of crying and fussing (you and the baby's). And when the crying and fussing doesn't go away and is making you absolutely nuts, just put him in his crib or bouncy seat and shut the door and walk away for five to ten minutes. It is during those moments when you will get a new understanding why Child Protective Services exists.

Nat, are you here and what doctor are you seeing on Monday? And when is your appointment? I will be there on Monday too ... just to see the nurse.

I am glad neither of you have noticed the widening of my ass. I hope nobody at the work picnic today notices either.

Anna woke me up at 6:15 this morning. Lovely. I need a nap.

In regard to your bathroom problems, are you taking Colace? Or FiberCon? You need to take something and try and eat an apple every day (I know that is difficult for you) and don't eat any bananas or cheese.

FiberCon makes it so that you go on a regular basis and Colace makes it so everything is soft ... you decide which drug you need, but take something before you have to buy Preparation H. Unfortunately, my friend Jamie and I have experience in this area. It isn't a fun day when that happens.

Sounds like all of our husbands are batting a thousand right now ... won't it be nice when things return to normal and they aren't total schmucks? At least I have you two who understand.

Delivering the Truth

Have you ever heard of being touched out or gived out? This theory or concept alludes to the idea that people have a slight irritation or are completely annoyed when meeting the constant needs of an infant or toddler. This happens because you are in constant physical contact with another human being. So when other people (another child or partner, for example) need something from you (whether it is nursing, snuggle time, play time, or sex!), you have very little left to give of yourself. People can have a feeling of their skin crawling or a tense and anxious feeling similar to nails across a chalkboard. This is why, when your partner grabs your ass and gives you a knowing wink, you want to judo-chop them in the neck ... or the nuts!

From: Natalie
To: Kim, Celeste
Sent: July 23

I'm here ... sadly. I go back to the doctor tomorrow at 4. My doc is out of town until the 6th so I'm sure the new doctor will not want to discuss induction.

I think my hemorrhoids are saving themselves to make a grand appearance during labor. Can't wait.

From: Kim
To: Celeste, Natalie
Sent: July 23

I am going to talk to the MD at my appointment in two days. Then I am going to run out to the store as soon as possible after that to buy some stool softener!

From: Natalie
To: Celeste, Kim
Sent: July 23

That makes me feel a little better about the bonding thing. Good to hear similar experiences.

Okay, fair warning, here comes a rant.

Let me also tell you girls (Celeste, you are probably familiar with this) about a little something called hostility. I am very fed up with my coworkers and family members seeming disappointed that I haven't delivered yet. I'm tired of people calling and asking if I'm still "on schedule" ... WTH?? I am tired of people telling me to have sex with my husband as this will apparently bring on labor guaranteed. (Another myth ... because it sure didn't work for some of us ...). I'm tired of people telling me "he'll come when he's ready" and asking me how I feel.

Yes, I'm a large and bitter woman these days. I don't want to talk about my cervix and my mucous discharge with everyone. I don't want to have sex with my husband. He certainly doesn't want to have sex with me (I'm not sure why not since I'm so charming and delightful these days). I am tired of snoring louder than any 500-pound man on the planet. I'm tired of my groin hurting so bad when I move in bed or try to get out of bed that it nearly brings me to tears. I hate that I had to grab the towel rack for support today when getting out of the shower and it ripped off the wall.

I AM A SHENORMOUS BREAKER OF TOWEL RACKS!

I am tired of wearing the same three things because nothing else fits—not that these three things fit, they just cover more skin than the other items.

I'm tired of not being able to feel my right hand. It makes holding things or typing or doing just about anything difficult. I'm very tired of lying around like Jabba the Hut and just waiting

... waiting for labor to start or my water to break or for some small glimmer of hope that I can have my body ripped in half and be done with this pregnancy. I'm also tired of restraining myself when Brad says, "I don't know what the big deal is ... it's not even your due date yet."

Okay, deep breaths ... going to my happy place.

How are you girls doing?

From: Celeste
To: Natalie, Kim
Sent: July 23

I will be at the doctor's office at 2:00 p.m. ... so hopefully, I won't still be there when you are there ... we would have a problem if that were to happen!

You will have to let me know how your appointment goes.

I am glad to know that you have finally hit that final stage of "get this damn kid out of here any which way you have to do it, or I will kill someone." Isn't that a pleasant place to be? Nothing makes you happy, nobody understands, and there isn't one nice thing you can find that is happening in your life. I wish for you understanding from your husband and labor (soon).

But while we are on the topic of TMI ... I have an issue that I didn't have with Anna and I am wondering if you guys have it too. I need to talk about lips—and not the ones on my face. If this is too much for you, just skip this upcoming paragraph.

I feel like mine are swollen. Like they are full of something—fluid, blood, whatever. But something that makes them big and swollen and, frankly, bothersome. Does anyone else have this problem? Do I need to talk to the doctor about this? Exactly how do you bring that up at the doctor's office? And John keeps telling me he needs to have sex. He just doesn't get it.

How can I have sex when I have a huge belly and my lips are swollen? Talk about uncomfortable!

Dr. Bob says

Sex in an uncomplicated pregnancy is fine as long as you physically and emotionally feel up to it. Only if there are certain complications occurring is it necessary to avoid sex. If you are concerned, ask your health care provider.

Although you may feel as if you are the only one to ever ask that question of your provider, it is asked every day. It is not uncommon for men to have concerns about what "damage they might do." Trust me, we men think we can do more damage than we can. It is okay in uncomplicated pregnancies for women to have orgasms; however, they will usually have some contractions after sex and orgasms. These typically will not cause preterm labor or harm. They usually fade away within a few hours.

Some complications, (but not exclusive) that would result in not having sex would be placenta previa, preterm labor, preterm premature rupture of membranes, or vaginal bleeding. Again, if you have a question, ask your health care provider.

From: Kim
To: Celeste, Natalie
Sent: July 23

I am not having any problems with my lips, but I did read that this is something that can happen. I feel for you though as extra tissue in that area cannot be pleasant. Ben came to me (guiltily) about two weeks ago and said that although he loves me very much and finds me beautiful, it totally freaks him out to think about having sex with me right now "knowing that she is in there." I told him not to flatter himself because he isn't THAT long and I don't want him touching me anyway.

So thankfully, I do not have him begging for sex, and the wise man has also not even suggested "other things" that could be done.

From: Celeste
To: Natalie, Kim
Sent: July 23

Oh how I long to have a husband that doesn't want to have sex and that is a bit creeped out about the whole thing. And the fact that yours has not suggested other ways of releasing his "tension" more than makes up for his yelling and screaming fit this weekend in the Old Market.

As for the lips, I am glad that you have read about this occurring ... then I won't bring it up tomorrow at my appointment and look like a total freak.

From: Natalie
To: Celeste, Kim
Sent: July 23

Celeste, I have the same problem as you do with the "lips." It has just happened in the last few weeks. I really hope things go back to normal after delivery; otherwise, I'm going to a plastic surgeon for some sort of nip/tuck.

On a different note ... we have fleas in our house. Brad and I both ended up with bites last night. I blamed it on the dogs (of course) until Brad told me he had been outside spraying for bugs and saw a "whole bunch of little bugs jumping around." So, yes ... my husband gave our dogs fleas.

We are having the carpets and vents cleaned tomorrow, as well as the house sprayed/treated. The dogs get dipped today and every piece of linen and clothing in our house (especially baby stuff) gets washed in hot. Good times.

From: Kim
To: Celeste, Natalie
Sent: July 24

Natalie ... u there?

On another note, I would like to share that my bathroom experiences are becoming increasingly less and less pleasant. My fear of hemorrhoids is now uncontrollable. Furthermore, whenever I empty my bladder I have about a minute of total discomfort. As in, someone must be squeezing my bladder and other internal organs as tightly as possible because I am in pain. I may just quit going to the bathroom altogether.

From: Celeste
To: Natalie, Kim
Sent: July 24

I have to admit that one of the MAJOR reasons why I think I am going to go ahead with the repeat c-section is because then I won't get a hemorrhoid (or poop) during labor ... is that pathetic?

From: Natalie
To: Celeste, Kim
Sent: July 24

Yes ... still here.
No, I think that is rational. I'd do the same thing.

From: Kim
To: Natalie, Celeste
Sent: July 24

After the strain of my bathroom experience this week, I am quite fearful of what will come flying out of me when I push to deliver.

By the way, did I ever tell you guys about the story that one of the Labor and Delivery nurses told me when I worked at the hospital? Well, if not, you need to hear this. I was mortified one day when I heard that women actually poop when they are pushing. How insulting to one's pride!

So then she goes on to tell me that during one delivery this woman was pushing and a long ole log came snaking out. She said that she watched it coming at her and the doctor was right next to her. He looked at her as if to say, "You take care of this one sista ... " and then she did a judo chop to the log.

Oh, God, please don't let this happen to me!

Dr. Bob says

In my experience, most if not all women are worried or terrified about pooping during labor! It is extremely common and is part of a normal birth process. It typically occurs during the second stage of labor, while you are pushing the baby out. It occurs when the baby is coming down and compresses or pushes on the rectum resulting in stool being pushed out.

If it is to occur, there is no way to prevent it. If it occurs, nurses, midwives, and physicians take care of it without saying a word. To be quite honest, we really don't even notice ... it is part of the delivery process. I believe that it often occurs without mom or husband even being aware.

Some women will try enemas to prevent this. Enemas can be quite uncomfortable, result in dehydration, and still not prevent pooping during labor. My advice: try not to worry. If it happens, know that millions of women have pooped in labor before and millions more will after you.

From: Natalie
To: Celeste, Kim
Sent: July 24

Yeah, thanks to that lovely story about the "ole log" of some poor woman ... I'm terrified. (And that really made for great dinner conversation by the way.) I'm certainly eating less and going more frequently these days ... I think my body is clearing the way.

From: Kim
To: Natalie, Celeste
Sent: July 24

I have finally admitted to myself that I am doing too much. Working till 6:00 every night and taking a class is too overwhelming. I am continuing to feel sorry for myself because the stupid furniture store has not gotten in the stupid rails for the boys' bunk beds so we can't start on the baby's room yet, which I would like to do so the basement is not full of her furniture and clothes.

Furthermore, I am starting to get anxious about how I am going to take two classes in the fall and it didn't help that someone close to me naturally assumed I would be missing more than one week's worth of classes after I deliver. I get home every night and feel like I have been totally wiped out. I plan to stay on my own personal pity party until my class is over this week and then I will reevaluate in a few weeks.

From: Natalie
To: Celeste, Kim
Sent: July 24

Feeling sorry for yourself is okay, I think. I'm feeling very sorry for myself at the moment. If you feel overwhelmed, then you have to cut back. I know that graduate school has been your priority for a long time, but if it takes you an extra semester or two to get through with your sanity intact, then that is what you have to do. I plan on continuing my pity party until I have my body back to myself.

I have to go chug some more soda since I haven't felt this kid move all day long. That is another thing. He hardly moves at all, which totally freaks me out. I feel like I should have a fetal monitor strapped around my belly at all times. I haven't carried this kiddo for this long for a tragic outcome, so I'm going to deliver a caffeine-addicted kid. What's the problem?

Dr. Bob says

With caffeine use in pregnancy, like most things, moderation is the best rule here. Though some women totally avoid caffeine during pregnancy, and that is fine, low to moderate amounts are fine. What are low to moderate amounts? Most would agree that up to 200 mg a day is considered low and up to 300 mg a day is moderate. [A Starbucks brewed coffee, grande size, contains 160 mg of caffeine.]

There has been some research that suggests an association with excessive caffeine intake and decreased fertility, miscarriages, and stillbirths. It should be noted that this research has conflicting results. However, most would recommend a cautious approach and recommend a 200 mg a day limit. It is considered safe to consume caffeine while breastfeeding. However, caffeine does get in the breast milk so the same recommendation applies.

 From: Kim
To: Natalie, Celeste
Sent: July 24

I too have noticed that I am getting a little nervous when I don't feel her for some time in the day. Especially since she usually is so active, I feel like she might come busting through any minute. One of my friends had the audacity to state that she had read somewhere it takes seven years to get your body back. I thought, "You bitch. Why are you telling me this?" Then I remember Celeste and another friend who this did not apply to so I am once again hopeful.

Delivering the Truth

Remember that pregnancy isn't an excuse to eat everything in sight. What goes on, must come off! For most women, your body isn't going to bounce back to its pre-pregnancy state after delivery. It takes a lot of hard work and planning to eat well and exercise, especially once you have a baby to care for!

From: Natalie
To: Celeste, Kim
Sent: July 24

I think it's all attitude. Sure things shift around and will never be the same, but you don't have to carry around a pouch for seven years. I plan on working hard to get some sort of a body back. I'm going to Jamaica in June. I have to be in a swimsuit. That is my motivation!

 From: Celeste
To: Natalie, Kim
Sent: July 24

Well, I am back from my appointment with the doctor, and I didn't have to bring up the lips issue because it got brought up by the doctor. I now have spider veins in my legs ... she wanted to know if I am having pain down there because apparently you can get varicose/spider veins in the lips. When you do, it hurts.

I told her that I have pressure and she said that pressure is different than pain and if I have pain, I need to let them know because some women apparently need to have them "taken care of" (I was afraid to ask how) before delivery. The nurse said I need to lie down with my legs higher than my heart and I could wear support hose (right, it is 90 degrees outside!). Apparently instead of a boob job, I am getting leg and lip work done.

So as far as getting your body back ... thank you for thinking that I had my body back ... I can tell you that when I was naked, it was obvious that I had a kid. Obvious to me anyway.

From: Kim
To: Celeste, Natalie
Sent: July 24

Wow! I had no idea that the lip thing could be that extensive. What good news for you to hear! Can you imagine if you were in the pioneer days and it was not right to talk to anyone about these things? You would think your body was going crazy! Now, you KNOW it is going crazy.

From: Celeste
To: Kim, Natalie
Sent: July 24

Okay. I really do have issues. I started freaking out after my appointment today.

Remember the movie *Fried Green Tomatoes* and the "Towanda!" segment? The movie with Kathy Bates? Remember how she goes to a self-discovery class with her friend and they get mirrors to look at their privates? Well, I did it. I needed to make sure I wasn't having vein issues in the lips.

I have vein issues in the lips. It is the most disgusting thing I have ever witnessed in my life.

I will be calling the doctor tomorrow morning to cry. I am mortified and humiliated. I know they have all seen everything before, but this is horrible. Why did I have to compromise and allow this pregnancy to happen? Men just don't understand how WRONG it is to be pregnant. There is nothing natural or right about this.

I am off to plug in a Disney movie and hang upside down from my toes.

Dr. Bob says

Varicose veins are abnormally enlarged superficial veins (closer to the skin). The vast majority of times these are primarily a cosmetic nuisance. Most often they occur in the thigh and leg, but can also occur in the labia and vulva. Hemorrhoids are another type of varicose vein.

Varicose veins are quite common and occur to some degree in at least 50 to 60 percent of women. Labial and vulvar varicose veins are more common than most pregnant women think. It has been reported that at least 10 percent will have them. In my experience it would be more common than that. They are much more common in multiple pregnancies (twins, triplets).

Varicose veins can cause swelling of the affected area, pain, itching, and discoloration. Almost always the labial and vulvar varicosities go away by themselves after pregnancy (within a month) with no treatment.

Varicosities of the legs, I'm sorry to tell you, typically get better but may not totally resolve. Preventive measures have been suggested. Some are support stockings, exercise and walking, elevation of feet while lying down, avoiding prolonged standing, avoiding excessive weight gain, and starting all of these early in pregnancy.

From: Natalie
To: Kim, Celeste
Sent: July 25

I think you mean my toddler will walk out one day. Good lord. Do they not know I'm 5 foot 3 and have (well had) small hips? Are they trying to make me have a c-section?

My friend said to just lie and tell them I'm seeing stars and getting dizzy so I can be induced. I'm about twenty-four hours away from chugging castor oil. Seriously, I Googled it on the Internet yesterday to see how much I'd have to drink to throw myself into labor.

Pickle juice! I remember that story. I should have brought a jar to work. I am just back to wearing the giant grandma pads and hoping that will take the first gush until I can get somewhere else.

And as for John. Seriously give that man the husband-of-the-year award. That was the nicest thing ever. I almost cried ... yes ... I'm also a freak of nature big fat crybaby. I watched exactly twelve minutes of the movie *Big Fish* last night and was crying as if there were no tomorrow.

From: Kim
To: Natalie, Celeste
Sent: July 25

Just out of curiosity, why do MD's strip membranes? Is it just to help speed labor along or is there another reason for it? I thought it was the first statement but now I am second guessing myself.

I am thinking of asking Ben to ask the boy's moms if they can keep their sons for a week when we come home. I am anxious about how the breastfeeding is going to go, and I don't want to have to sequester myself in the bedroom every two or three hours. It is only one week ... not forever. Is that unfair? That will be my ONLY time to be a first-time mom and not have to worry about the other kids' needs.

Dr. Bob says

Is there any reliable way to start labor? There have been many reported methods to bring on the onset of spontaneous labor. To date, none have been found and verified to be reliable or reproducible.

Some of the examples are anything from acupressure, acupuncture, reflexology, drinking castor oil, intercourse, lots of walking, nipple stimulation, eating certain food, and many others you've heard at the baby showers. Obviously some are more fun than others ... at least for husbands, but none routinely work.

Many, if not all, will result in contractions, but these are generally short lived and not resulting in labor. Unfortunately. In regard to sex, it is completely safe as long as your water hasn't broken and your doctor gives you the okay.

From: Natalie
To: Kim, Celeste
Sent: July 25

The stripping of the membranes is to supposedly stir things up and it often puts women into labor. Not this one ... but other, normal, calm, rational women.

I don't think it's too much to ask to have a week to yourself to get your routine down. I agree 100 percent. I am going to have a house full of my family and Brad's family. I'm sure I will be insane, suicidal, and homicidal. I know everyone is excited and wants to help and they are coming from a good place, but I think everyone forgets how totally overwhelming this whole thing is.

I hope your step kiddos can take a week off and everyone can just deal with it. It is, as you said, your one and only time to be a first-time mom. I'm sure their moms had a week or more to themselves when they brought their babies home.

Dr. Bob says

Stripping membranes is a procedure that can be done by your health care provider in the latter stage of the pregnancy to "ripen" the cervix. It is not typically good or indicated to induce labor, but rather the indication is to ripen the cervix—that is, to help the cervix become more favorable for labor to occur.

Most studies have shown this to be safe and effective in appropriate situations. It is done during a vaginal exam. The examiner's finger is placed in the cervix and is used to separate the bag of water from the side of the uterus. It can result in some discomfort and cramping during the exam. There may be some spotting afterward as well as contractions. It should not result in significant bleeding or significant prolonged pain. In some situations it would not be indicated.

 From: Celeste
To: Kim, Natalie
Sent: July 25

I don't think I signed up for this—the whole thing I mean ... Because really, even after the baby is born, I didn't really sign up for anything that is happening or that will happen during delivery or that this baby will bring. I signed up for a one-year-old child and then for a twenty-year-old child. Nothing in between or before.

 From: Natalie
To: Celeste, Kim
Sent: July 25

Yes, yes ... I know. I signed up for a newborn, about a five-year-old then a college student ... not pregnancy or anything before or after. I feel I was duped.

From: Kim
To: Natalie, Celeste
Sent: July 25

I can honestly say that I knew what I was getting into after the delivery simply because I came into the picture when my youngest stepson was a year and a half and the oldest was six. So I have been blessed to see the different stages that these boys continue to go through.

I think it is time once again to talk about the things we are grateful for. This may be somewhat harder this time but let's give it our best.

1. I am grateful that I have the opportunity to complain about being pregnant because a million women would trade places with me in a heartbeat.

2. I am excited to see what she is going to look like.

3. I am excited to hear her little girl voice calling for me ... at the right time of day and not a thousand times in a row.

4. The bunk bed rails came in yesterday so I am grateful that my husband can't let anything sit for more than four hours so the bed is now set up and I can start the baby's room.

5. I am grateful to those wonderful people who have the courtesy to look at me and question if I am really almost eight months instead of five or six.

6. I am grateful my dad is going to babysit.

From: Natalie
To: Kim, Celeste
Sent: July 25

This is hard today.

1. I am grateful that I became pregnant and carried a baby

for this long without major complications. Many people would give anything to be in my situation.

2.   I am grateful for Brad. For all his quirkiness he makes me laugh out loud and he has not looked at me and vomited yet. I also don't think he's having a torrid affair although I could hardly blame him because he certainly isn't getting any at home.

3.   I am grateful for my family and friends who have supported me unconditionally through this.

4.   I don't know if I'm grateful for this or not ... but for the people that say, "Natalie, you look great." I, of course, don't believe them but it is awfully nice of them to say.

5.   I am grateful that we are ready to bring this kiddo home.

6.   And lastly, I am grateful to have funny friends like you two that I can gripe, whine, and bitch to and you don't call Child Protective Services or file a Board of Mental Health Petition on me for being an unfit parent.

 From: Celeste
To: Natalie, Kim
Sent: July 25

Ready to hear about my privates? I just got off the phone with the nurse.

First, she laughed at me. When I started off the conversation with "I have problems," she replied, "Well, I know that, but you have new problems?"

I said, "Well, aside from my mental health problems, I have veins in the wrong places problems." I proceeded to tell her the story of the horrifying mirror experience. I told her that I laid down all night with my toes resting on the ceiling and that things seemed better this morning when I took a quick glance, but there were still issues there ...

My prescription from the nurse is this:

- NO squatting, lunging, picking up heavy things or straining to lift anything.

- NO sitting or standing for long periods of time or she will put me on a restricted work schedule.

- Buy underwear that has spandex in it and wear it tight but probably not tight enough that it rips like Kim's experience. ☺ She also said that some women wear a maxi pad and that helps keep extra pressure down there too ...

She said that at my next appointment I need to remind her that I "want the doctor to take a look." I told her, "I don't want him to take a look! I don't want anyone to take a look! This is the most disgusting thing I have ever seen! It is horrifying!"

She again laughed and said, "You have no idea the disgusting things we have seen. This isn't one of them." If it gets worse or more painful or doesn't get better with the hanging by your toes from the ceiling routine, then I am supposed to call and see someone else in the office.

I didn't sign up for this.

From: Natalie
To: Kim, Celeste
Sent: July 25

I guess I am also grateful for our nurse! She has to have heard it all although I'm sure that my medical history is far worse and more terrible than everyone else's ... and that the weird things that are happening to me have never happened to anyone else. She is so freaking nice.

Well, good advice. Can you lift Anna?

I had to have the doctor check me and I didn't die. I thought I might but I didn't. I'm not to the point that everyone says you get to ... you know where you stop caring who sees your privates. I don't think I ever will. I guess I'd rather have the doctor take a look than the husband.

Did she say you should not engage in activities with John?? Maybe if the room is PITCH BLACK ... and he promises not to look it would be okay ... this coming from someone who all out refuses. So many people have said, if you want to go into labor you have to have sex with your husband. Nope, no way. He is not seeing this enormous body naked ... good thing we are both agreeable on that.

From: Kim
To: Natalie, Celeste
Sent: July 25

At this point I really don't think there is anything that I can say that would make you feel better. Veins are wrong—no doubt about it. If it makes you feel better, I am now noticing some things myself. I believe I was conveniently lying to myself before.

My issue is this: there have been times (recently) when I have been walking around and say to myself, hmmm ... you must be a little damp or sweaty today cause everything seems to be rubbing together. This morning I finally admit that it may be due to the fact that some things are more engorged then they used to be.

What's worse is that my boobs are getting stretch marks again. I tried on a strapless bra that I had to see if I could wear a really cute shirt for our date night last week. I figured it might be a skoshe small since it was a "C" and it was a little roomy for me prepregnancy. When I tried it on, it looked like I was trying on a size A. I really realized exactly how much I had grown after I did that.

Everyone keeps telling me to enjoy it but how can one enjoy it when they stick out and get in the way? Every time I eat something, it falls down my cleavage. Furthermore, if they are this big now, how much are they going to sag after the pregnancy?

It looks like all of us are going to have to invest in some plastic surgery after this.

From: Natalie
To: Kim, Celeste
Sent: July 25

Absolutely things change. Let me tell you a little something else that is horrifying. I have read that as things down below become engorged, they may swell or turn dark red. Try white.

I decided to check things out yesterday before my appointment to make sure that the crop circle was aligned with Jupiter and Mars and my skin has turned ... pasty. This can't be good. I thought maybe I have an infection or something. But at the MD she didn't say one word about it as if it is normal. Great.

My maternity pants that I've been wearing since about twenty-four weeks are now busting at the seams. I think they are only holding together because of a hope and a prayer. My boobs are not necessarily getting much bigger girth wise ... but I'm now wearing a 38 instead of my normal 34. I think I gained six pounds last week. My kid is going to be 15 pounds and a world record holder.

From: Kim
To: Natalie, Celeste
Sent: July 25

I always feel so much better after reading these emails ...

Well, I can no longer laugh directly at Natalie but must laugh with her. I have now had my own food experience that does not quite compare to Natalie's taco experience but probably shocked innocent bystanders nonetheless.

It all happened on a beautiful summer day. I left work to go to class. Of course, I am ravenously hungry and am ready to gnaw off my arm when I pull into McDonald's. I am a good girl and only order a hamburger, fries, and soft drink instead of a Big Mac. There isn't much time between work and school, which means that I have to try to run my pregnant butt from the parking garage to the building.

We all know that my professor is a dear woman who does not mind if we eat in class. So eating before getting to class was not the issue. No, sadly, it was my overwhelming need to shove food into my face as quickly as possible. So this is the picture I made today ...

Pregnant woman half running/waddling to class. Hands full with purse, book bag, soda, and bag of food. Hair was flying as I am shoving multiple french fries into my mouth. I imagine that those I passed heard the snorting noises I made and dodged the french fries that were flying all about (although not many as again, I was HUNGRY!). And, of course, since my hands were totally full I am holding everything super close to my face making me look even more obscene.

It humbled me ...

From: Natalie
To: Kim, Celeste
Sent: July 26

I love to greet every morning with all my coworkers stopping by my office saying, "You're STILL here??" It really makes me happy.

Did you guys know that pregnant women are supposed to be drinking 3 to 4 liters of water a day? Holy crap! I thought I was doing awesome by drinking one. One of the residents told me that today.

Dr. Bob says

How much water to drink during pregnancy? A good guide is to drink half your body weight (in pounds) that many ounces of water a day. So if you're 150 pounds, that's 75 ounces. However, this can be affected by climate and level of exercise.

From: Kim
To: Natalie, Celeste
Sent: July 26

First I would like to say that there is something wrong with me. I talked to my MD yesterday and kindly explained that sometimes, after I go pee, my internal organs that are squished below my uterus (God only knows which ones those are) hurt. Sometimes they hurt so bad I have to stand there for a second or go lie down and scrunch my body up.

This morning, I felt pain even without going to the bathroom or having the urge to go. MD is running my urine to check for a bladder infection but I don't think that is it because it doesn't burn and it doesn't hurt all the time. Frankly, I'm tired of it.

Then, total humiliation. I am standing in the kitchen, by myself fortunately and I sneeze. Concurrently, I had a gusher. Yes, girls, I peed my pants. It went running down my legs. Not all of it, mind you, but certainly not a few drops. So I had to disinfect the floor, change my clothes, and cry that I am most likely going to have to have some type of female surgery after this is all over so I don't pee my pants every time I sneeze.

Natalie, I suggest you post a sign each day on your door that reads, "Today is _____, yes, I am still here. Kindly don't remind me."

From: Natalie
To: Kim, Celeste
Sent: July 26

I bet you have a UTI of some sort and the symptoms are just different because your guts are squished right now. That is easily corrected. As far as the loss of urine, that is also normal (I say this to make myself feel better because it happens to me). In my second trimester I would be done going to the bathroom and stand up to pull my pants up and ... um ... leak. That's when I started wearing the panty liners or pads. It's not a big deal. You have a human being compressing your bladder. I recommend the thin maxi pads.

I like the idea of the sign, Kim. I'm thinking of taking Monday off. The thought of any more full work weeks makes me want to jump in traffic ... if I could jump, that is.

From: Celeste
To: Kim, Natalie
Sent: July 27

Nat—you haven't responded to an email since 11 a.m. yesterday. I am afraid to ask if you are there—I am hoping I get no response to this email ...

From: Natalie
To: Kim, Celeste
Sent: July 27

You silly girls! Don't you know I will be pregnant forever? In fact, I'm quite sure you will both have your children before I do.

I feel like I have a volleyball between my legs ... but I'm still here. I am surrendering and taking Monday off. I keep thinking it's pathetic that I'm taking the day off ... but oh well. It's one less time I have to rotate my three work outfits I guess.

I had one contraction last night ... it woke me up. I got up and walked around and discovered my shorts were wet but I'm pretty sure I probably just peed myself. It's such a glamorous time in my life. TOWANDA!

From: Natalie
To: Kim, Celeste
Sent: July 27

My friend said that I should call the doctor's office and tell them that I'm feeling increased pressure (the volleyball). I told her I don't think I need to call unless I'm bleeding or my water breaks. What do you guys think? I guess I think this feeling is normal as things progress (HAHAHAHAHAHAHA) and with the bulging bag of water and all ...

 From: Kim
To: Natalie, Celeste
Sent: July 27

I guess my only thought is regarding the fact that when you woke up during the night you were wet. How do you actually know you just peed your jammies? I think if there is any question about that then you should call. Are you leaking at all today?

 From: Celeste
To: Kim, Natalie
Sent: July 27

I agree with Kim. If you had a bulging bag, but his head was engaged, you could have just had a "leak" of fluid but aren't getting the gush because his head is blocking the fluid.

Maybe just go down to L&D and ask them. If you are wearing a pad, they can just test the pad to see if the wetness is urine or amniotic fluid ... and you don't want to walk around being ruptured because you could get infected.

From: Kim
To: Natalie, Celeste
Sent: July 27

By the way, what did your contractions feel like? In the back or front? Painful or simply irritating? Inquiring minds want to know.

Also, I expect a full report after you do deliver. Hold nothing back. This is what any good girlfriend would do.

From: Natalie
To: Kim, Celeste
Sent: July 27

The contractions feel like menstrual cramps to start with, then radiate to my back. People say it feels like a squeeze ... it feels like cramps to me ... but they do radiate over my entire belly after they start.

I think it's just pee. Of course I'm wearing a pad and there has been something on it every day (pee).

The nurse from L&D told me to squat and bear down and my water will likely break. I'll save that for when I'm at home. Wouldn't I be contracting if I was ruptured?

From: Celeste
To: Kim, Natalie
Sent: July 27

No. My friend ruptured when she was at home and didn't contract for like six hours or something crazy. And then she went from 1 to 10 centimeters in forty-five minutes. No time for an epidural. She had to go au naturale. She initially thought she wet her pants, but then thought ... umm ... maybe not. She only had a small bit of fluid leaking after the initial rupture. She just wore a pad and never had to change the pad during her six hours of no contractions.

Are you sure you want to rupture at home? I think I would prefer to do it in a Labor and Delivery room or in the bathroom there at the hospital. That way you (or Brad) don't have to clean it up.

Anna has discovered bar soap. She thinks it is totally cool and gets all lathered up (including her hair). If she were not my daughter, I would think this was cute ... well, it is now noon and I have not been able to go anywhere because the girl won't get out of the damn bath. She has been in there twice now and is walking around the house naked in case I reopen the bathroom door ... She is a total pain in the ass and has her own brain. Why can't she be a follower instead of a boss?

 From: Natalie
To: Kim, Celeste
Sent: July 27

I think I'll see how the rest of the day goes. I had some shooting pain in the Va-J-J area, so I came to my office and Googled it. It said it's likely my cervix opening. Holy crap. I'm going to be complete before I have any freakin' contractions.

Well, for now, I'll bear down over the toilet. I don't want anyone here to have to clean that up. I'd rather clean it up myself. Plus, if my water did break at work I'd want to go and get my stuff. There are the everyday items that I can't pack until I'm ready to go, ya know?

As for Anna, it's funny, you have to admit it. And you know the answer to your own question. She's a boss because you are her mother.

Okay, it's time for a new cheer ... since it worked with the dilation.

Here we go contractions, here we go
Let's get it started—let the water flow
CONTRACTION—ACTION
CONTRACTION—ACTION
Let's see amniotic fluid not just pee
Let this kid come out and see ...
That it's fun on the outside
FUN FUN FUN on the OUTSIDE
Yeah CONTRACTIONS

Delivering the Truth

If this is your first rodeo, you believe that every little twinge, mucous-y discharge, urge to pee, or random physical change is a sign of impending delivery.

 From: Kim
To: Natalie, Celeste
Sent: July 27

Natalie, I think you should say you don't feel well and go home. Squat over the toilet and see what happens. If you have a gusher then I would pack your things and head back into work. Am I the problem solver or what! I have to admit I am rather jealous that you are this close (and by close I mean it still could be several weeks, oops, I meant days!)

Can I somehow just fast forward? Ben was all excited that we were two months away yesterday. It didn't enthuse me too much. Two months seems like forever and it is so freaking HOT!

From: Celeste
To: Kim, Natalie
Sent: July 27

Are you trying to say that I created the monster two-year-old that I have? Damn. Another good reason to chuck the whole pregnancy thing and adopt. Poor Anna has inherited the worst of me and John. She is a boss, she has her own brain and insists on using it, she is an extremist, she pushes things to the limit, she loves chocolate and ice cream and would eat them nonstop until she puked ... the poor girl is an addict already. Just wait until she is old enough to try drugs and alcohol. John and I are screwed.

The new cheer is pretty good. I did like the first one better, but I understand that the creative juices just aren't flowing as quickly now as they once were. Let's just hope the cheer is good enough to get the contractions going. I think it might be.

As for where to rupture, can we just vote for no rupture at all? Because really, there isn't a good place to do it ... anywhere. The whole birth thing is really too messy. Couldn't God have figured out a cleaner way?

Delivering the Truth

Remember your precious little bundles of joy will grow up and have their own brains and personality. They will have their own ideas about Every. Single. Thing. Man, there should be a sequel to this book!

From: Natalie
To: Kim, Celeste
Sent: July 27

No, you created a child in your image. I said nothing about a monster.

You guys were the cheerleaders in high school, so where are your creative juices?

Rupture, membranes, fluid, it's all a terrible process. Whoever said this is the most natural thing in the world was obviously smoking a doobie.

From: Natalie
To: Kim, Celeste
Sent: July 28

I think my water may have broken although I've convinced myself I just peed my pants. I got to my office this morning and sat down. LOTS OF PRESSURE ... like when you wait too long to pee. I COULD NOT stand up. Otherwise it would have been disastrous. I rolled my office chair into the bathroom. YES! I did a lightning flash ninja move to remove the pants and transfer to the toilet. With minimal spillage I made it! It kept coming. I couldn't stop the stream. It wasn't a fast gush or anything but a steady stream far after I felt relief. It was also cloudy like I couldn't see the bottom of the toilet. So I called the nurse in Labor and Delivery. She said put a pad on and wait a half hour unless I'm having contractions. I'm not. I felt him wiggle around this morning. She said that if it's amniotic fluid it has a distinct smell—not bad just not urine smell. So I'm waiting. I called Brad. He wants me to go check in now. I want to go home because of course I didn't shave my legs or nether regions since my MD appointment last week.

Holy shit! Is this it?

 From: Celeste
To: Kim, Natalie
Sent: July 28

Holy shit! THIS IS IT!

 From: Kim
To: Celeste, Natalie
Sent: July 28

Oh my gosh! I just read these emails! What is going on?? Have you heard anything??

From: Celeste
To: Kim
Sent: July 28

I called the hospital and she isn't there yet. I talked to one of the nurses I know and she said that Natalie called down there to ask if her water broke, and they told her to come down, but she hasn't showed up. I don't know anything more. I will call or email when I hear something.

From: Celeste
To: Kim
Sent: July 28

I called again and she is there. Brad answered the phone and immediately gave the phone to Nat—and that was not a good idea. She was contracting while she was trying to talk to me ... She had no idea how far she was dilated or anything else that was going on ... so that is all I know at this point.

Waiting ...

Waiting ...

Waiting ...

From: Celeste
To: Kim
Sent: July 28

She delivered! Kim, I will call you with details and we can decide when we want to go visit.

 From: Natalie
To: Kim, Celeste
Sent: July 29

Thanks for stopping up. It was great to see you guys. Sorry there was no time to chat ... I really wanted to share with you what happened. It was a bit crazy if you ask me.

Delivery:

Okay, so after the possible water breaking incident, I decided to go home. I felt "weird." I wasn't in pain or anything but I just felt weird. I closed my office door and called my boss and told her I was going to go home and see what happened. So of course as I'm walking out my entire department has to see me and ask me what was going on.

I called my sister and told her what was going on and that she should call my mom since she lives five hours away. I got home and got in the shower. I felt I needed to shave the legs and the nether regions—just in case.

By the time I was out of the shower I was feeling pretty crampy. I was moving really slow as I was packing the last few items in my suitcase. By the time I was zipping up my bag I told Brad that I thought we should get going to the hospital. I felt like I had to go to the bathroom. I swear I sat down on the toilet five times for nothing.

He was in no hurry at all. In fact when we got in the car we sat in the driveway for about ten to fifteen minutes while he finished up a phone call for work. I was feeling pretty uncomfortable at that point, but I didn't say anything. Brad told me he was just going to get me settled at the hospital and then he was going to go back to work for a while.

My mind was kind of dull at this point. I was just staring at the clock trying to time my pains. When we were about fifteen minutes away from the hospital I was becoming increasingly uncomfortable. Brad was busy on the phone and driving and then asked me how far apart my contractions were. I timed them ... two minutes apart. We then started going warp speed. I became fearful for my life. I told him to slow down. I still wasn't sure if I was really in labor yet.

We got to the hospital and I swear there were eighty cars waiting to park. I told Brad to do valet parking. He JUMPED out of the car and threw the keys to the valet guy and yelled, "We gotta go. She's in pain." I love that guy!

So, we walked in. I had Brad look at my pants to see if they were wet. He said no. I had to stop at the bathroom again—nothing. I looked at my pants in the mirror. They were wet.

I got upstairs and everyone was so excited to see me. I still told them I wasn't sure if I was in labor. We got checked in and I was asked to put the gown on. I did and crawled in bed, still embarrassed to be there and expecting to go home. We didn't even bring the suitcase in because I knew we were going home. The nurse came in to check me. She lifted up my gown and then said, "Um, Natalie ... you have to take your underwear off." I didn't know. Besides I'm not in labor! So off to the bathroom again to change.

Then she checked me. I was ruptured, dilated to 5 or 6 and about 90 percent effaced. This was it! I was in labor. I was staying. I was staying.

Then I started getting REALLY uncomfortable. I became all wiggly, I could not keep my legs from moving around. It felt like hot, electric cramps. That is the best description I can come up with. I guess I thought the pain would be in the vaginal area ... nope.

This is about the time that you called, Celeste. I didn't mean to be rude but I could not even think straight. I was really hurting. My sister arrived and she and Brad were blabbing away while I was dying.

The nurse came in and asked if I wanted an epidural. HELL YES WOMAN! She said it would be about an hour before they could come and offered me stadol. She said it would relax me in between contractions. I said no. Then Brad and Angie were staring at the monitor saying stupid things like, "Wow, that was a big contraction. Did you feel that?" and "That contraction was really small compared to the other one, huh, Natalie."

I was ready to kill someone. I would have killed them but there wasn't enough time in between contractions to effectively wrap my hands around their necks. I thought I better get the stadol to help me not kill my family. Then, my dad, stepmom, and five-year-old niece arrive. They all want to hang out and chat. I was trying to be nice but asked them to leave. I couldn't stand the noise in the room.

At about noon (two hours after we checked in) the planets aligned and the anesthesiologist arrived for my epidural. I leaned on Brad while they snaked the catheter in my back. It hurt and it made me jump a little bit but I was ready for pain relief.

I was still in pain—but less. They checked me an hour later and I was complete and ready to push, so I think my body was just dilating faster than the epidural could get to my pain.

By 1:30 I was supposed to start pushing. They put an internal monitor on him and the doctor said, "I can see blonde hair." I ignored that. Clearly she didn't know what she was talking about.

His heart rate kept dropping. It made me nervous. They put me on oxygen and made me lie on my left side. Brad did an excellent job of lying to me and telling me it was fine and I was doing great. I was having a hard time coordinating my breaths and pushing. I was totally numb so I couldn't feel the contractions or if I was pushing in the right spot and making any progress.

I remember saying something really stupid to my doctor like, "This is just like golf. You have to get your swing coordinated to hit the ball." I swear everyone in the room stopped and looked at me like I was a complete moron.

After about an hour and a half of pushing the doctor wanted to let me rest and "labor down" ... whatever that is. So I rested and Brad went out to give my family an update. I still didn't want to see anyone.

After about an hour the doctor came back in with some very scary looking equipment and said something like, "We are going to quit messing around and get this baby out."

Apparently his heart rate was declining and they were in a bit of a hurry. She told me they were going to use forceps. I didn't care. I was getting nervous. I could hear his heart rate beep... beep ... beep.

I kept looking at Brad. He being a brilliant man again and lying to me telling me he was fine and I was doing great. They placed the forceps in. Remind me to write a strongly worded thank you note to the inventor of the epidural.

One push and his head was out. No heart beats. I couldn't hear anything on the heart monitor—FREAK OUT. I became super woman with one more push and he was out and on my chest.

He was here, he was alive, he was perfect, he was mine, he was a baby and he was mine and he was alive and I delivered him! I DELIVERED HIM!

After a few minutes of me crying and shaking and freaking out I said, "Meet Gage James everyone." My healthy, perfect, platinum blonde son was here. It was the best feeling ever! The doctor must have known about our abnormal quad screen and all the perinatologist visits because she immediately looked at me and said, "Natalie, I don't see any signs of Down syndrome." Brad and I looked at each other and knew it was all behind us.

They took him over to the warmer to clean him up. I had to pry Brad off of me and remind him to get pictures. I could hear my family on the other side of the door saying, "We hear crying!"

Brad was talking to me like it was a normal day. And then I started shaking and cramping again—placenta delivery. That was kind of uncomfortable mainly because they had to do a manual exam. I think that meant they crawled in there and examined me with a flashlight. That's what it felt like anyway.

After that fun was over, the doctor started sewing me up. I had a third-degree tear. While they were sewing me up, Brad took our perfect son into the hallway to meet the family. After about forty-five minutes I was back in one piece.

They put Gage in my arms and asked me if I wanted to feed him. "Sure, how hard can it be?" They raised up the bed and I remember feeling really good. I remember seeing Brad across the room. He started getting up and I hear, "HEY SHE'S PASSING OUT."

Yep, I about dropped our kid. I passed out with him in my arms. They caught him. By the time I came to there were lots of people in the room staring at me. I was so embarrassed for fainting. They kept asking me dumb questions to see if I was oriented. I was fine.

I tried to feed him. He wasn't really into it and I found out I don't know what the hell I'm doing. A little while longer they wanted to move me to postpartum. I stood up to pivot to the wheelchair and passed out again. Again—very embarrassed. They said it was probably a combo of the meds, lying down all day and the blood loss. I finally made it to postpartum and got to see my family.

Meet Gage James
Born: July 28th at 4:56 p.m.
Weight: 7 pounds 0.9 ounces
Length: 20 inches

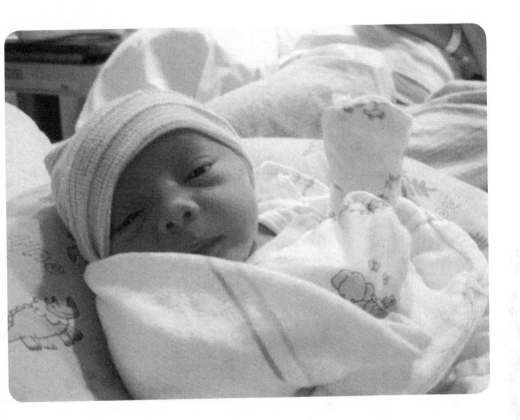

Dr. Bob says

During delivery, many events occur. Let me make some sense of some of these activities.

Monitoring during labor ... to adequately cover this is beyond the scope of this book. However, in general there are two methods of monitoring contractions and a baby's heart rate. They are external and internal monitoring. The majority of labors are monitored continuously. External contraction monitors can tell when a contraction occurs and how long, but tells nothing about the strength or intensity. Internal contraction monitors tell us about the contractions plus the strength and resting tone of the uterus.

Fetal (the baby's) heart rate monitors are also used either externally or internally. External monitors use ultrasound waves, and internal fetal monitors have a direct connection to the baby. Typically, the internal monitors are considered more accurate, but external monitors are often all we need.

Let me address perineal lacerations or tears. They are incredibly common. It has been reported that up to 90 percent of ladies experience some degree of laceration during delivery. Most lacerations (these are tears) occur in the perineum, which is the area between the vagina and the anus. A first-degree laceration is a small skin deep tear, which either heals on its own or may need a few stitches. A second-degree laceration (tear) is deeper, tearing the skin and muscle of the perineum. This requires stitches.

More extensive tears, third—and fourth-degree, occur in about 9 to 10 percent of deliveries. Third-degree tears extend down from the vagina to the anal sphincter, which is the muscle that controls the anus. A fourth degree results in tearing from the vagina into the rectum. The repairs of third and fourth degree require more care and time, and often post-delivery measures.

Now, on the subject of epidurals: They are a safe and effective method for pain relief during labor, and we offer them a lot. Often the anesthesiologist is the laboring mom's best friend. However, with this said, occasionally an epidural will not relieve all the pain and there may be certain areas or sides that pain relief is noted to be less effective. Overall, epidurals are very safe, result in good pain relief, and are extremely common.

Why do women faint after delivery? Passing out can occur after delivery for different reasons. The most commonly recognized reason is when a woman feels faint. After blood loss, the blood flow does not always get to the brain as well as it should, so ladies feel faint, lightheaded, shaky, and even pass out.

Gradual measures should be taken with movement after delivery to try to avoid this. Another less commonly recognized reason is called vasovagal episode. This can occur when the vagus nerve is stimulated through things such as dilation of the cervix or other causes. It results in a dramatic response of the mother passing out. It usually goes away in about thirty to sixty scary seconds, but it appears mom is not breathing, her heart rate slows down, and her blood pressure decreases. When moms come to, they behave normally.

From: Celeste
To: Natalie, Kim
Sent: July 31

Are you getting any sleep?

I hate to say that I took a nap today. Don't want to make anyone jealous.

What was the first night like? I remember coming home with Anna and thinking ... "Now what?"

I felt like I had no idea what I should be doing. It just felt very strange. I really wanted to take the nurses home with me because I knew I wasn't qualified to take care of a baby.

You have to let us know once your relatives leave. Kim and I will bring over dinner and celebrate. ☺

From: Kim
To: Natalie, Celeste
Sent: July 31

I would just like to say that I am on the phone with the baby store with a complete idiot. Somehow, a different baby monitor showed up on our registry that we did not register for. The other one that we wanted was taken off. I couldn't fix it online so I have to call this idiot and she does not understand what I am saying.

Patience, young Skywalker.

I am interested in what is going on with your life, Natalie. I swear! Just needed a little narcissistic me time.

From: Celeste
To: Natalie, Kim
Sent: July 31

How hard is that to figure out? I don't want this monitor, I want another one. Just switch it, moron! The heat must be getting to that person's brain.

From: Natalie
To: Kim, Celeste
Sent: July 31

Hello, ladies. I was discharged on Sunday at about 5:00 p.m. We got home and had three couples and two kids over at our house—they brought dinner. It was nice to see everyone and I guess I'd rather have them all in one shot than scattered through the week.

It was just stressful because we literally had to throw all the stuff from the hospital in the nursery and they were there. I looked like total shit and was not moving around very well.

Since we had a house full of people, the dogs were outside and didn't really get to be around Gage to get used to him. I got my second wind after everyone left and started putting stuff away, signing him up for insurance, etc. Then I put the bassinet in our room and tried to go to bed.

Jackson (the mastiff) would not leave him alone. With every sniffle or whimper from Gage, he was trying to peek over the top of the bassinet. So I locked the dog in the bedroom and took the bassinet out to the living room and slept on the couch.

I was totally high on drugs and lack of sleep because I got spooked in my own house—and by Gage. I was on some good

T3's (fun painkillers!) and Gage's eyes were very wide open and it started to freak me out (bad acid flashback, I guess). I only got about an hour of sleep.

Today my mom came over while Brad ran some errands. I wanted to go to Target and get some nursing bras and such. When he got back, my mom and I went to Target. The checkout guy asked me when I was due ... always good for the ego. I didn't care. I do still look pregnant and I had a cart full of baby stuff.

He is feeding better and I hope my milk comes in by tomorrow—living on colostrum can't be very fun. The first few minutes of every feeding is enough to curl my hair—it hurts so bad!

My friend, who is a nurse, called to check on us tonight. I told her that he hadn't pooped since we left the hospital. She said that concerned her and that if he doesn't poop by tomorrow I need to take him in. My mom, sister, and Brad were here and I told them (my mom and sis) that they needed to leave because they don't fold our laundry right and they aren't putting the dishes in the right places from the dishwasher.

Then I had to go into the bathroom and ball my eyes out for starving my child. I guess these are the baby blues. Wowza!

He just had a really good feeding. I still can't get him to burp. Brad is the master burp-finder. So I'm feeling better and more chemically balanced. My mom and sis stayed for dinner and forgave me for being a total freaking, crazy bitch.

I'm going to go take a sitz bath—or my version of aiming the shower sprayer in strategic locations and get a few hours of sleep. I'm feeding him every two to two and a half hours. That's all we can muster right now.

All in all, I adore him. I just think he's the sweetest thing ever. I feel guilty for not feeding him right or that he's peed through his gown and blankets three times today (obviously I'm new to the diapering).

My mom, sis, dad, and my stepmom are hovering. I just feel like I don't always have a place for them or something for them to do. But they come over and hang out and it's always fine. Brad's mom and dad are both coming to town next weekend. Brad's mom made a bunch of dinners and stocked our fridge. Wow, is that the best idea ever. It's so nice to just grab something and heat it up.

Brad is being amazing. He is a great dad and is very watchful and protective of me. Usually I would find this very annoying but I'm totally comforted by it. Bottom line—it's totally worth it. I know no one will tell me if he's ugly, so I'll never get a truthful outside opinion, but I just think he's the greatest. When he looks around for me when he hears my voice or smiles (probably gas) ... it's just the cutest thing I've ever seen. I'm not a sappy person, but I'm forever changed by this experience.

We have an appointment with the pediatrician on the 14th for a well-baby checkup and she is going to recommend someone for a kidney ultrasound to make sure that polycystic-what-cha-jigger thing is cleared up (the opening duct in the kidney that both my OB/GYN and perinatologist thought was cleared up, oh well).

I have a lot of thank you notes and emails to respond to, but it's slow going for me right now. The nether regions are still swollen and sore and my feet are still pretty swollen. I'm still waiting on the first postbirth BM. I've loaded myself full of Colace and Milk of Magnesia. I hope it won't be too traumatic.

I'll let you know a good time for the visit/dinner, probably the second week of August would be best. I have to learn how to work the car seat!

Okay, girls. I appreciate you listening to me ramble. I've got a sitz bath with my name on it.

Delivering the Truth

We strongly encourage you to think extremely hard about visitors coming to your home immediately following your discharge from the hospital. Know your limits! Share them with friends and family *before* you deliver. How you feel about visitors before you deliver (Sure! Come on over!) may be drastically different after you deliver (Give me my baby and leave me alone!).

August

From: Kim
To: Natalie, Celeste
Sent: August 1

I think this has been one of the most helpful emails to date. It is so awesome to hear how enthralled you are with your son! I can see why you are worried about starving your son, so when I starve my daughter I will remember your feelings and do my best to blow them off. Your feelings on all of your visitors have confirmed my thoughts of not wanting a bunch of people over.

From: Celeste
To: Kim, Natalie
Sent: August 1

Has your milk come in yet? If so, how fun is that?

I kind of feel like shit today—heartburn and allergies. I had to take two allergy pills. Think that will do something to the kid? My right eye is starting to swell and is all red. I am so sexy right now it is amazing.

Nat, fill us in on the whole feeding thing when you have a chance ... and how are your hormones?

From: Natalie
To: Kim, Celeste
Sent: August 2

Yesterday was the most traumatic day I've ever experienced in my life. It is going to be WAY TMI ... beyond TMI. Good lord ... sit down for this one.

At the end of my last email I told you that I loaded myself with Milk of Mag and Colace. Well, yesterday afternoon I started feeling crampy like it was time for the BM. I went into the bathroom ... cramps got worse but nothing happened. Then the cramps got so bad I could barely stand up. My instinct was to stand up because it hurt so bad to sit down.

Gage was sleeping, thank God, because I was in the bathroom for an hour and a half. I called my mom and asked her to come and sit with him. I could barely stay on the phone. This is my theory of what happened.

I hadn't had a BM since Wednesday or Thursday of last week (mind you it is Wednesday today) ... so there was already a problem in the shoot. What I passed was bigger than anything that has ever come out of me. I was crying and biting a towel. This is not sarcasm. I was really biting through a towel ... it was TERRIBLE!

I made a huge mess in the bathroom with blood and yuck. All I could do was heft myself into the shower and BAWL MY EYES OUT. I cried so hard. I cleaned up the bathroom and put everything in like four trash bags and set it outside of our house. Poor, poor Omaha Sanitation. The next time I peed it came from a part of me that pee should not. So, tearfully I called the doctor's nurse and told her what happened. She told me to come in this morning.

Brad took me to the doctor today. I did rip some stitches and there is a little start of skin breakdown, but she didn't want to repair anything for fear of making the skin breakdown worse. So I'm on an antibiotic, I have to pack the wound ... which means I have to look at it ... it's terrible and the hole I'm aiming for is not really recognizable so I just pack everything and hope for the best.

I go see her again on Friday afternoon and I'm supposed to soak everything (sitz baths) like four to six times a day. Who has time for that?

I took Gage to the doctor and had them look at him because I was convinced that his bilirubin is like 25 and he's dying. They were not concerned at all. All in all ... I feel much better today. He's not dying of renal failure and he's getting enough food ... he finally pooped early this morning. With my new feelings about poop it was hard to be happy about it ... but I was.

Long story short, start Milk of Mag daily in like your thirty-sixth week along with your daily Colace. You need to keep everything soft. Who cares if it's too soft ... no one should have to go through what I went through. It was worse than all the contractions I had ... worst pain of my life. Please take this advice and share it with your girlfriends.

I'm terrified of the bathroom still, but my doctor is the best doctor in the world. She gave me a hug, which about made me cry again. I feel like I might have post-traumatic stress disorder from this incident. Physically I hope I'm on the mend. Hormonally? I really thought I wouldn't be hormonal ... I was wrong.

That's all I have for now ... go, run, now! Get your Milk of Magnesia. It tastes terrible ... but drink it and like it ... never, never bitch about it. It is your friend ... your best friend in the entire world.

One more item. To add to my woes, I started pumping with an old pump that I borrowed because I freaked out that I was starving him and tried to give him formula. He wouldn't take it. I called the lactation consultant and she gave me some good suggestions, calmed my worries that I was starving him, and encouraged me to hang on—avoid the formula and pump. I've been getting 1 to 2 ounces every two to three hours. It's not much ... but at least I know he's getting something. I am now pumping and feeding him to try to make more.

Delivering the Truth

It is probably time to address and acknowledge that we had no idea what the hell we were doing! If you are hoping to breastfeed, ignore everything we say in this book except this: Call the La Leche League in your area and consult with a lactation consultant. We have had so many breastfeeding friends comment about how they feel as if they are starving their baby in the first week or so of life because they have no idea how much breast milk their baby is getting. It would be so much easier to have a lactation consultant come live with you for the first two weeks after delivery! However, if that isn't possible, we found this book to be very helpful: So That's What They're For! by Janet Tamaro.

From: Kim
To: Natalie, Celeste
Sent: August 2

I have tears in my eyes I feel so bad for you. Do you remember how I went on and on about my BM last time and you two told me to go get Colace? Well, your bathroom experience sounded similar like mine but without ripping stitches (I feel so bad for you on that). My legs went numb from sitting on the toilet and Ben could hear me moaning and gasping for air. But, if you are like me, your next BM won't be near as bad.

To me, it sounds like the pumping/breastfeeding is going well for you. Newborns only take about 2 ounces every two to three hours anyway so you are right on track. And it sounds like Gage is doing great or otherwise work would have rushed him off to the NICU and called Child Protective Services on you!

I am way too emotional today. Celeste already knows, but my horse had to be put down this afternoon. It was a terrible experience and I have never seen a horse in that much misery. Her poor body was all banged up and bloody from thrashing around and falling all through the night. I have been with pets when they were put to sleep but this is not something I want to experience again. Most horrible was when she fell against the barn and got stuck so we had to rope her feet and pull her over to her other side. Try doing that with a thousand-pound animal that is in severe pain and be eight months pregnant.

It sounds like between you, me, and Celeste we have had a totally shitty last day or so ... no pun intended.

Dr. Bob says

Constipation after delivery is not uncommon. It occurs in up to 20 percent of moms. It can be due to many reasons: dehydration, lack of eating, pain meds, fear of pooping due to pain or stitches, and slower digestive system from labor or surgery. Do not have fear or worry; the stitches will hold. Hydrate well, eat a high fiber diet, and take advantage of the urge.

From: Celeste
To: Natalie, Kim
Sent: August 2

That is quite possibly the worst thing I have ever heard! Oh My God—I am so sorry that happened to you. The good thing is that your doctor was so awesome. You have just totally confirmed my decision for a repeat c-section. I know that bad things can happen to my incision, but I think I would rather pack my belly than pack down there!

Regardless, I am adding Milk of Mag to my Target list. But packing and skin breakdown? How do you pack down there? And after all of that trauma, is it ever going to heal? How much time are you taking off from work? I would think it would take at least twelve weeks to heal that ... wow.

But at least you now know that Gage isn't starving to death. Anna wouldn't take formula either—especially if I was on the same floor of the house. She took it when I wasn't home once and when she was in the basement and I was in our bedroom. She wouldn't let me feed her a bottle even with breast milk in it. It had to be someone else. The first time she actually ate a bottle with formula with me nearby was at her baptism (when I wasn't going to whip out the boob) when my friend Jennifer (Anna's godmother) fed her the bottle and sat right next to me. She was about four weeks old.

After delivery, I didn't think I would be that hormonal, but Oh My God. I have never had hormones like that before, and I have never cried that much before in my entire life. The sad thing is that I didn't feel like I could admit it to anyone—at least you are admitting it to us. I hate to tell you that if your experience is anything like mine, the hormones are going to get worse before they get better.

And the sleep deprivation will do strange things to you—so take a nap!

From: Kim
To: Natalie, Celeste
Sent: August 2

Okay, now I am crying again.

From: Natalie
To: Kim, Celeste
Sent: August 3

Well girls, I thought I should warn you—safety first.

So far I feel lucky to get a shower. Where does the time go? If he sleeps eighteen hours a day then why can't I get everything done? Weird.

Ok, everyone quit crying—jeez—what happened to the heartless, sarcastic women we once were?

From: Kim
To: Natalie, Celeste
Sent: August 3

Glad you are doing better! Now on to me.

I have noticed in the past week that I am having discomfort on my left lip. Yes girls, you heard me correctly. Although that is not entirely accurate as I have attempted to massage the area to locate the exact spot of the pain and cannot.

I mostly feel it at night when I roll over and it feels like I have pulled a muscle or ligament in that area, but you would think it would also then be tender to the touch if I had. I also will feel discomfort if I am sitting and my pants get a little bound up in that area. Anyone have this problem themselves?

And for the record Celeste, I had my own Towanda experience and did not see any veins whatsoever. *sigh* Two more whole months.

I also have my plan of action in place. I am going to slowly up my dose of Colace (whether I need to or not) the week or two before I am due as well as gorge myself on fiber. I am hoping this will prevent my previous experience or Natalie's dreaded experience after delivery. The only thing I worry about is becoming so "soft" that I actually have a major liquid blowout during delivery. What are your thoughts? ☺

Dr. Bob says

Symphysis pubis dysfunction is a pregnancy condition in which the ligaments that hold the pelvic bones aligned during pregnancy become too relaxed and stretchy. This can result in the pelvis feeling unstable. It is felt to be due to a hormone (relaxin). It can result in your feeling as though your legs may not work or fall out of place, your pubic bone pulling apart, pain in your hips, pelvis, groin, and rear.

It is rather common, being reported to some degree in up to 25 percent of pregnant ladies. Typically, it goes away by itself after delivery. However, there have been reports of about 5 to 7 percent of moms having continuing symptoms after delivery.

From: Celeste
To: Kim, Natalie
Sent: August 3

As for the nether region concerns, I don't know what your problem could be since you don't have any veins. It seems a bit strange that you can't nail down the exact problem.

Maybe you should go to the myofascial release therapist I went to on Wednesday. That was interesting. Definitely some form of voodoo. I felt like I should have been in California or Sedona getting the "treatment." Which is fine with me, but I am not sure exactly how often I am supposed to get the voodoo treatment and what exactly is supposed to happen. I need to ask Jennifer's neighbor who is the one who suggested I get the voodoo treatment in the first place.

Anyway—how to avoid Natalie's disaster in the bathroom. I say that, Kim, you need to up the fiber and if the Colace is working fine to keep it soft enough, don't increase that. Too much Colace isn't a good thing ... but too much fiber isn't bad. But maybe you can relay the horrific experience to your doctor and see what she says. She may have a plan for you to avoid this.

From: Natalie
To: Kim, Celeste
Sent: August 4

Well, in my opinion, crapping on a doctor or a nurse is a far better choice than ripping your stitches out alone—without an epidural, in your own bathroom. I agree with Celeste. Don't overdo the Colace. I took one a day during pregnancy. I'm sure if I would have upped the dose to two a day I would have been in much better condition.

I have to go back to see the doctor today at 2:30. It might be my first outing with Gage alone. I want to take him to meet everyone at work ... but don't know if I can manage it on my own. I'm a little nervous. What if he freaks out? I guess I'll have to do it eventually.

He's still doing great. He wakes up every two to three hours and wants to eat, look around, cry, poop, and pee and go back to sleep. What a life. We gave him his first sponge bath (at home) last night. The nurse at work warned me that I might become emotional during it since they cry so hard. I laughed at the time.

Well, I didn't cry right then, but it was really hard to watch. Luckily Brad thought it was funny that he was freaking out and took the lead and got the job done.

Another crying spell last night ... I tell ya ... the shower has become my new place to cry. I was having some physical pain last night so I took a bath/shower and cried. WTH?? Then I laid down for a nap last night (about 9:00 p.m.) and could not fall asleep. I kept thinking about the delivery and how scary it was and it went so fast ... I guess I just haven't had time to mentally process the whole ordeal so I'm doing it piece by piece. I'm sure that doesn't make sense. Well maybe to Celeste. I think we are going to have some more interesting conversations after you guys deliver.

As far as breastfeeding, I'm so glad I didn't start feeding him formula. It's SO MUCH EASIER to be the food machine. He doesn't spit up and it's far less messy. I try and pump one time a day so Brad can do a feeding ... and it's always a total mess for both of them. He has the hiccups after almost every feeding (from me or bottle) but I've read that is normal and it doesn't hurt them.

Do you guys have the book *The Baby Book*? It's written by a doctor and nurse (husband and wife) ... it's so awesome. It has everything in it and it reads like an owner's manual. Totally my type.

Don't worry girls. You are both in the homestretch. Yes it's totally easy for me to say that and I had very bitter feelings in the end at people who told me it will be anytime ... and he'll come when he's ready. Jerks. I'm trying not to be a jerk ... just encouraging. ☺

Delivering the Truth

It is important to talk about what your ideal delivery looks like. However, it is equally as important to talk about all the possible scenarios that could happen. Your delivery will likely fall somewhere in between. If your delivery is not what you expected or you feel like you need to process your feelings surrounding your delivery, there are support groups out there. Google them to find a group near you.

From: Kim
To: Natalie, Celeste
Sent: August 4

No plans to overdo the Colace as I am taking one a day right now. But if I don't have a bowl of some type of fiber cereal every day then I pay for it so I am thinking about upping it to two per day starting in September if things don't get better.

I am glad the breastfeeding is working out and glad to hear that you are pumping and Brad is bottle feeding as that is what I want to do as well. Too bad about the baby blues, but I guess that is one more fun thing we will all have to endure.

From: Natalie
To: Kim, Celeste
Sent: August 6

My lowest point yet. You know I've been seeing my doctor to keep an eye on my broken ass. I saw her on Wednesday and Friday of last week. She checks everything out ... irrigates it and tells me I'm doing okay. She gives me a hug at each appointment and makes me laugh and I thank God for her. Best part of the appointment is I lost six pounds in two days ...

Lowest point of appointment and maybe my life ... As I was lying all splayed out on the examination table and the doctor was helping me up when she was finished, things kind of shifted and I farted. It wasn't a huge fat man fart ... but it was certainly audible. I didn't even laugh or cry ... simply put my head down like a beaten dog and said excuse me.

She said, "Well that's about par for the course." I'm not sure what that means exactly ... either I'm so gross she expected me to fart and ruin her life and mine or she realizes I've had such a hard time that this doesn't even phase her. Either way, if I could move to Antarctica and live in a cave, I would.

Having a baby ... $14,000.

Ripping your episiotomy stitches out while pooping ... $1,200.

Farting in stirrups and being able to share it with your friends ... PRICELESS.

Good lord!

From: Celeste
To: Natalie, Kim
Date: August 6

This is very funny. I know you don't want to hear this, but I almost ruptured a vein laughing at this story. I know it was horrible to live through, but at least it happened with your doctor—the most wonderful and understanding woman in the world. She will likely forget about the whole thing because, believe me, after all the nasty women she has seen, this is a minor thing.

She knows how embarrassed you were/are about it and also knows you didn't have any control over that. She knows you aren't like my husband who chooses when and where to fart and always aims his butt in the direction of my nose like a fifth grader. I am sure I will have a horror story to tell when I have to show my doctor my beautiful veins.

From: Kim
To: Natalie, Celeste
Sent: August 6

Oh dear God! That is sooo funny! This totally beats my experience of walking to a clothing store from my car and ripping a HUGE man fart. I didn't know it was coming. It just happened. I was so mortified I stopped in my tracks and looked around to see if anyone was nearby. There was only a guy about half a block away but I am sure he heard it.

I feel so much better now that I have heard your story! I wonder how women manage not to let five thousand go when they are pushing that baby out.

Dr. Bob says

Tooting in pregnancy is not only normal, but universal! Almost every new mom thinks she is the only pregnant lady to have gas, and she's afraid to ask about it. It is due to the hormone progesterone and the fact that your GI tract slows down. This increase in gas causes no problem for the baby or you ... just maybe those around you.

 From: Natalie
To: Kim, Celeste
Sent: August 6

Today I got a nap. It was like heaven. I must sleep really hard when I do get the chance because I'm in a total fog right now.

My friend let me borrow her old ass breast pump ... did I tell you guys this? It's an antique. It only has one speed that works and you never know if you are going to get the "so slow don't even bother speed" or "suck your eyeballs out through your nipples speed."

So I press start while gritting my teeth and hope for the best. It's terrible. There are tons of used pumps on eBay so I'm bidding on one. It's not like any of the parts that touched a stranger would touch me, it's just the actual machine. I never really understood the inner workings of a breast pump but now that I have this antique one, I get the concept and understand the need for a great one.

About the family, my sister was REALLY good about only coming over when invited—even though it killed her. My mom hovered but I felt okay telling her to let me have some time. Brad's mom is here but has plans to hang out with Brad's sister and some of her friends for some of the time.

From: Celeste
To: Kim, Natalie
Sent: August 6

I got a Charley horse in the middle of the night on Friday night/Saturday morning. It was so bad it woke me out of a dead sleep—and woke John too from my freaking out. I drank water and ate a banana but I don't know what else to do ... it still hurts!

Nat, you had experiences with Charley horses didn't you? What did you do and did they still hurt thirty-six hours later?

Hormones? Any more crying spells in the shower?

From: Natalie
To: Kim, Celeste
Sent: August 6

I had the same leg cramps that woke me up from sleep ... there is nothing you can do but grin and bear it. Eat bananas, drink extra water ... I think it's just one more joyous thing about pregnancy. Obviously Baby Snodgrass needed a hit of potassium and stole yours. I guess you could call the nurse and see if there is a supplement you could take.

I also started drinking milk. I hate milk but liked a glass a few times a week when I was pregnant ... that seemed to help too. Or maybe it was just in my head.

We have more family in town (Brad's mom and dad). I was exhausted last night. People were holding Gage and he was screaming and it took all I had not to snatch him away from them and run down the street. GIVE ME MY CHILD!! HE WANTS ME!!! Other than that kind of internal monologue freaking out ... I've been okay. No more crying ... just feeling really tired and pissy. Is that hormonal or just normal for me?

Feeding is going MUCH better. I try to pump at least once a day. This hasn't happened for the past two days because of family but I am trying to stock up. I have been sleeping on the couch so as not to wake Brad up with the crying baby, but with all the house guests I have been staying in the bedroom this weekend.

Brad says it wakes him up. I think I'm being totally quiet. I don't know ... I don't want to live on the couch for twelve weeks but it seems so much easier. We'll see. I hope he (Brad) will get used to the sound of me and Gage and learn to tune it out.

I've also picked up a little trick that helps. You are supposed to rotate sides to start feeding on ... well in the middle of the night I can't remember so I've been switching a ring from hand to hand to help me remember what side to start on. I also read that some moms use one of those rubber bracelets for the same purpose ... very handy.

Dr. Bob says

Muscle cramps of the legs are very common in pregnancy, especially the second half of pregnancy. They tend to be more common at night. No specific reason has been well worked out in regard to why muscle cramps occur in pregnancy. There are no conclusive treatments. There is some data to suggest increased hydration, magnesium supplement, calcium supplement, or B complex (B1 and B6); however, there are conflicting results. It is recommended to discuss any supplements you want to take with your health care provider first.

From: Kim
To: Natalie, Celeste
Sent: August 6

I have Charley horses all the time ... especially if I squat down during the day. I drink milk daily and have bananas during the week. On a happier note, my nether region pain is going away slowly, which makes me believe I did pull something. On a sadder note I found stretch marks. They are on both sides of my ass and are purple. At least they are in a spot that can be hidden at this point.

Good idea on the ring thing. Does your wedding ring fit again? As for Brad ... I say sleep wherever you are comfortable and if he gets woken up momentarily—oh well!

I can tell from the "sound" of your email that you are feeling better! Thanks for the validation on limiting visitors the first week for their own safety and well-being.

I would like to say that last night was possibly the worst night of my life. I had my first baby shower, which went great and Ben's family was very generous. We got a lot of big items which really helps out! I also got the cutest baby book so I am excited to go home today and try to remember dates of when I first found out I was pregnant and the first time I felt her move. I have a feeling that is how this book will be done after she comes too.

Now the bad part. I started feeling sick to my stomach around 10:00. My heartburn was ferocious. When isn't it though? I stacked about three king-sized pillows on top of each other and threw my feather pillow on top for good measure. I lay there for about an hour willing myself to get some sleep.

I then had the most terrific pain shoot across my belly and it tightened up. I thought about digging my nails into Ben's flesh to ease my own pain but thought perhaps I should be a real woman and suck it up. So I went into the bathroom (the place I now typically dread to go) and sat there for forty-five minutes with the wonderful experience of my legs going numb.

I had this happen probably three more times, and each time it did my stomach made a peculiar gurgling noise. Do you think that anything happened? Nope, just felt a little better after a while so I got up and went to bed where I had a fitful sleep the rest of the night. Needless to say I am exhausted today.

I would also like to add that since I discovered my beautiful stretch marks on the topside of each cheek yesterday I do believe they are multiplying in numbers by the second and turning darker and darker purple. I knew my butt had expanded but I had no idea that it seemed to have grown to such a magnitude that it required stretch marks to prove it.

Dr. Bob says

Heartburn and reflux during pregnancy: More than 50 percent of pregnant ladies suffer from heartburn. It is more common in the second and third trimesters. Many changes that occur during pregnancy result in heartburn. The good news is that it almost always goes away after delivery.

To help prevent or ease the heartburn, try eating several smaller meals instead of three larger meals. Avoid foods and drinks that result in heartburn (for instance, caffeine), don't lie down or recline immediately after eating, and elevate your head when lying down. Also, there are several over-the-counter medications to talk about with your health care provider and if it persists, prescription medications.

 From: Celeste
To: Natalie, Kim
Sent: August 7

Sounds like your night was as good as mine. I was up from 4:30 a.m. onward because Anna thought it was time to get up and play. I finally got her to go back to sleep around 6:00 a.m. At that point what was the point in me going back to sleep? My alarm was set for 6:45 anyway.

Yesterday I did get to lie around much of the day and noticed a significant improvement in my veins last night ... but I also felt like a big fat lazy cow. I am shocked I don't have stretch marks on my ass too. Your stretch mark story prompted me to inspect my body and I am still in the clear ... for now. I still only have the dark veins all over the "other" place. Cute.

From: Natalie
To: Celeste, Kim
Sent: August 7

I made it through without any stretch marks. I brag about this because I still have a huge gut and I ripped my ass—so I feel I deserve to be spared at least that.

I had another crying spell this morning after thinking about the delivery. I seriously think I'm still processing it. It was so wild and like nothing I've ever been through ... words fail me. They are good feelings, not bad, but I think I didn't have time to be scared so that is what is coming out.

Right now I have him asleep on a boppy on my lap while I type ... pretty fancy. I should be in the shower while he's asleep but I've never been very good at time management.

I think I'm going to take both of us to the chiropractor tomorrow if I can get myself together in time. I'm sure we are both out of whack—especially him after the forceps.

I bought a new breast pump on eBay last night for $150 + $13 for shipping. It comes with the receipt that shows it is seven months old. Pretty good deal, I thought.

Off to feed this little guy and maybe get a shower in.

 From: Kim
To: Celeste, Natalie
Sent: August 7

Shower?! Why shower!? Please, you can go at least two or three days and spray yourself with flowery stuff without smelling like people who smell like dirty socks. You're fine!

I am hoping that my friend's pump isn't too old. Then again, her kids are all under three so how old could it really be? I think you got a major deal on the pump! Did you do your victory lap around the house yet? That may shed off one more pound (good job on the whole six pounds by the way!).

One more note. This made my day. My mom-in-law had asked how much weight I gained so far (twenty-seven pounds as of two weeks ago). She said wow! She knew two young gals that gained fifty and sixty pounds. I was so gleeful I could barely contain myself but was able to say, "Oh really?" They are both rail thin and about ten years younger. It's the little things in life that make me feel good.

Dr. Bob says

Weight gain in pregnancy—like it or not, it is inevitable and necessary. However, eating for two doesn't mean eating twice as much! There is no one rule for weight gain during pregnancy. It depends on prepregnancy weight and BMI, your health, and your baby's health.

Some general guidelines are 28 to 40 pounds for underweight women (BMI < 18.5), 25 to 35 pounds for normal weight women (BMI 18.5 to 25), 15 to 25 pounds for overweight women (BMI 25 to 30), and 11 to 20 pounds for obese women (BMI > 30). Probably as or more important is the food eaten to achieve the weight gain. Eat fresh fruits, vegetables, and protein. If you have questions, discuss it with your health care provider. [BMI is body mass index, which is a measure of body fat. You can find BMI calculators online and plug in your weight and height to find a current, non-pregnant BMI.]

From: Natalie
To: Kim, Celeste
Sent: August 7

I am showering every day. One, because I have to hose down the southern hemisphere several times a day anyway, and two, it makes me feel more like a human and less like a milk machine. I hear ya though ... as soon as all this company leaves I can't guarantee daily bathing.

I think I got a good deal too, and I hope this pump works better than the pump I have borrowed. I didn't do a victory lap ... I should have.

Let's discuss co-sleeping. How many women have I counseled on co-sleeping? But really after getting up with him three and four times during the night, by the third go around he doesn't want to go right back to sleep so I've been lying him next to me. I'm such a light sleeper these days I can hear him breathe. I know it's not a good idea ... but it gets him a few more hours of sleep and me too. Don't call Child Protective Services on me.

I always enjoyed the stories of so and so gaining a million pounds during her pregnancy. Relish in the moment. I think I'm going to start walking around the neighborhood next week. I think three weeks after delivery is a reasonable time to get the butt moving ... as long my doctor thinks I won't jostle anything loose.

Kim, as far as your abdominal pains, I have no idea. I certainly had some weird pains but nothing that caused me to nearly die or clench Brad's skin until he bled. Maybe a phone call to the OB's office is in order.

From: Kim
To: Celeste, Natalie
Sent: August 7

I think it was gas pains to be honest. Since I am not having any today, I am going to keep it between us three gals.

Thirty-three weeks tomorrow!

From: Celeste
To: Kim, Natalie
Sent: August 7

Co-sleeping. I did it with Anna—only in the twin bed in her room, not in our bed. It completely freaked John out to have her in our bed because he is such a hard sleeper.

I think that I would like to get one of those little divider/space maker things that you can get to put in a bed and then put the baby in it ... that way the new baby is still in bed with me for easier breastfeeding, but I will feel more like a decent parent by having a separator between us.

I spoke to the nurse today, and she said my iron is low (not a shock) so I am on iron pills now. She asked how my veins were. I told her yesterday was good because I could lie low all day but today is a different story.

She said, "Well, the doctor is going to want to look at those and you need to tell us if they get worse because they can get pretty painful."

I told her that I knew they could get painful because they hurt when I stand up. She said, "Well, if they are hurting already, then I can pretty much guarantee you by the end of your pregnancy he is going to put you on a restricted work schedule."

I don't think she understands what my work schedule is actually like, but I am sure she means that I need to be lying on the couch feeling like a fat cow much more than I am.

I can't believe you (Nat) are finding the time to shower and spray down the nether region at least once a day with all of your family and taking care of/feeding Gage. You are supermom and should be commended. This is an incredible task.

As for the breast pump, way to go! When you are finished with that, you need to send it my way ... you can even "rent" it to me. I am all about pumping much more this time than I did last time, which was almost never. ☺

 From: Kim
To: Celeste, Natalie
Sent: August 7

I saw a cute little bedside bassinet that goes next to the bed and has a lowered rail on one side. I keep thinking I should register for it. There is absolutely no way I can bring the baby to bed as Ben falls asleep as soon as his head hits the pillow, and he throws the blankets and pillows to kingdom come. He does not wake up to the sound of a bullhorn or me screaming at him to roll over before I smother him with my pillow due to his disturbing nocturnal sounds.

What the hell ... I think I will register for it and if I get it, then bonus! Otherwise it is walk my happy ass to the baby's room every night three or four times.

From: Natalie
To: Kim, Celeste
Sent: August 9

I have low iron also. They said I was borderline needing blood in the hospital … but the doctor decided not to order it. That is fine with me. I'm on iron supplements now too. I do feel a little puny sometimes.

The co-sleeping. I feel okay when he is on his stomach on my stomach … but sometimes I have laid him next to me (on his back) and gone to sleep. I am less comfortable with this because he tends to turn toward me and it's just dangerous and a dumb risk to take. I need to get better at setting him in the bassinet without waking him up.

We'll see how the pump works. I should be getting it this week. Brad was shocked when I told him I planned on breastfeeding just through my leave. I actually told him it's a day by day thing … who knows if I'll be able to do it tomorrow. I don't know what he was thinking.

I really think three months is MORE than adequate. What are you guys thinking as far as duration?

From: Celeste
To: Kim, Natalie
Sent: August 9

Breastfeeding: I plan on breastfeeding as long as I can stand it. And then once I go back to work (at around six or seven weeks) I will start to wean. Obviously with my flexible schedule, I can still be home and breastfeed even though I am technically working. But I also can't easily pump if I have appointments or have to teach all day.

Let me tell you, even though you think you will be able to pump at work, you can't. There isn't enough time in the day. It is my opinion that if you breastfeed for two days, good for you. If you breastfeed for longer than that, you rock. If you breastfeed for over a year, there is something wrong with you (ha ha, yes, I am over-exaggerating here).

I was totally fine with Anna sleeping on my chest also. It was the lying next to me thing that also freaked me out, but I was sooo damn tired that I couldn't help it sometimes. There were many a day that John would walk into Anna's room and say, "Uhm ... Celeste? You have Anna in bed with you and a boob hanging out ... " because I fell asleep feeding her.

I have a pedicure appointment today at noon. Yea me! Gotta have pretty feet for Okoboji. Anna and I leave on Friday and come home on Tuesday.

From: Kim
To: Celeste, Natalie
Sent: August 9

Yes, please ... hold your applause. I mean it now, you must stop you're embarrassing me. It is true, I gained only one pound since my last doctor's visit. I have to admit I almost made a beeline for a jumbo Goodrich malt afterward but did restrain myself to only stopping at Sgt. Pfeffers for the chicken salad. I felt this was appropriate since I always gorge myself on it and then have major gastrointestinal issues later and right now I could use some assistance in that department.

My next appointment will involve "The Cervical Check." I can't say that I am looking forward to this, and now I will definitely have to set up my waxing appointment as I have stalled far too long now. Wouldn't want to show up as a wooly mammoth or *gasp* go into labor and actually DRIVE MYSELF HOME TO SHAVE FIRST! I'm not mentioning any names here, Natalie.

Now I have a confession. I have to admit I did a little (a lot) of eye rolling as you two spoke of all the possible ailments your kids had/have. You were a tad over the top for me on some of them. But I noticed I am getting highly anxious these last few weeks that something is going to happen and we went all this way only to have a major crisis.

Last night I really began to worry as she wasn't moving like she normally does when I go to bed. I sat there and jabbed my belly so much I think I probably caused some type of brain damage or at a minimum bodily bruising. I can't have this type of anxiety in my life right now ... can't I just skip forward to delivery without putting myself through this for the next seven weeks?

In addition, my parents were all excited as they spoke of an article they read in the paper last week about belly Band-Aids—made especially for pregnant women who have developed "outies." Just exactly what were they trying to say? I do not have an "outie." Why even bring this up in my presence? I'm still trying to deal with the fact that I have stretch marks on my ass for goodness sake!

Dr. Bob says

There is no absolute as to when cervical exams are done in pregnancy. Typically, one would be done at the beginning of the pregnancy. After that the most common time to start checking the cervix would probably be about thirty-six weeks. However, some providers may do that more and some less. The information can assess if dilation has occurred, if the cervix is thinning, if the cervix is softening, presentation of the baby. If you have a preference about the exams, I would recommend talking with your health care provider.

From: Celeste
To: Kim, Natalie
Sent: August 9

How did you do it! You need to share. I need to hold myself to one pound so spill it! Congratulations. I envy you and your one pound.

From: Natalie
To: Kim, Celeste
Sent: August 9

One pound is awesome! I never remembered what my weight was at my last appointment but I knew I was gaining multiple pounds in between. WOOOHOOO!

My belly button never popped out ... it just stretched to its max and looked kind of flat. Weird. Gage lost his belly button this morning. It started coming off yesterday. It was a little bloody and weepy.

I, of course, freaked out thinking we had ripped it off and his guts were going to fall on the floor so I had to call the nurse at work and ask her about it. She said clean it with alcohol at every diaper change. Today it just looks raw but much better. Weird ... I guess I thought it would just come off and look like a belly button.

We went to the chiropractor yesterday. Gage got adjusted ... he is a little out of whack from the forceps. My chiropractor took pictures of him being adjusted and wants to make it a poster on his wall ... Gage's first modeling job. I told him our people would call his people. HA! No, I said, "OF COURSE YOU CAN!" So, we have to go back in a week or so to see if he is better aligned. He says it should help him sleep, digestion and boost his immune system. I also got adjusted ... it felt great. I'm a fan of the chiropractor.

Brad's mom made us a bunch of food and left this morning. Really, again ... that is the most helpful thing anyone can do.

My doctor has suggested to me soaking in cool baths or, of course, the good old shower sprayer for ten minutes strategically pointed where you need it. It has helped me. The swelling is finally going down ... I think anyway.

About "The Check." I thought it was going to be terrible, but it wasn't. For some reason or another I warded off the check until I was thirty-seven weeks and I lost the dreaded plug the next morning. So I thought it was a good thing. It is really quick and a bit uncomfortable ... not painful.

As far as the shaving, I don't regret my decision to go home while in labor. It made me feel more comfortable ... I mean ... people are staring right at you for several hours. You might as well clean it up as much as possible. ☺

As far as the freaking out about the health of your baby, I think it's totally normal. I'm sure Celeste and I are on the fringe as far as excessive freaking out, but I think it's totally normal to worry about any changes (such as movement). Like I said the last four weeks when he barely moved at all I had to drink a soda every day and make him move ... otherwise I convinced myself something terrible had happened. And I was always so relieved to hear the heartbeat at my doctor's appointments.

From: Kim
To: Celeste, Natalie
Sent: August 9

I was just talking to someone last night who said that studies are coming out now that show babies who visit the chiropractor show less colic and sleep better. Moms are supposed to have better deliveries if they have been going (I need to get my stretch marked butt in there pronto!).

I think I am going to have to up my Colace to two a day. Ben laughed when I stated that I seemed to be "getting rid of" huge Sequoia trees, but I am dead serious. My poor, poor bottom.

From: Natalie
To: Kim, Celeste
Sent: August 11

Just when I think I'm doing well and in a good routine, I hurt so bad I think I'm going to die. I actually cringe when he wakes up and needs to be fed. I am hoping my new pump arrives soon so I can try to pump and see if that is less painful. The kid has a death grip!

Also, I have learned something important. Do not try to pull away from the baby while he is feeding ... you have to insert a finger in his mouth to "break the seal." Otherwise you will curl in a ball and cry for days.

Who said this is the most natural thing??

From: Kim
To: Celeste, Natalie
Sent: August 11

I am now totally convinced that I will fare much better if I deliver this child out of my ass as opposed to other routes since this area is significantly stretched out and damaged already. (TMI—I know!) I did read that tip about "breaking the seal" in the Amy Spangler breastfeeding book ... and now I will definitely remember it!

I am so annoyed with everything lately. I know this is hormones or something, but it sure makes me feel better to think that every living organism out there is idiotic.

From: Kim
To: Celeste, Natalie
Sent: August 14

I have a new very best friend. I met her on Saturday and am considering starting a short-term affair with her. She gave me one of the best massages I have ever had and I must add that her pregnancy table was extremely comfortable!

When I had my massage at the school, the bed didn't quite fit me right and I actually felt a bit dizzy when I got up. I could have stayed on her table all day long! Plus, she gave me a deep tissue massage that didn't feel like one. I know that she really worked on me because the next day I was actually sore but while she was giving me the massage it didn't hurt at all. It was a beautiful thing.

On a more dismal note, I am definitely not feeling the baby move as much, which is totally freaking me out. I am going to monitor the situation for another day and then I am calling. I still feel her move ... just not as much as before and my doctor said that I should feel her move just as much but it won't be as extreme. This is not the case. I will try not to get too freakish about this situation.

From: Natalie
To: Celeste, Kim
Sent: August 14

I am not a massage person ... it's been proven again and again. I'm glad you enjoyed it though.

I'm also glad to see you become a bit freakish about your pregnancy. It makes me feel better about mine. As I've said I felt the need to caffeinate my kid to assure myself he was still hanging on in there.

We went to the pediatrician today. Gage has gained a pound and grown an inch. WOW! I guess my mammary glands do work. He is 70th percentile for height and 30th for weight. She said he looks great and was very impressed with his growth. Yahoo! He's healthy.

I have another appointment with the doctor tomorrow to recheck the southern regions.

From: Natalie
To: Celeste, Kim
Sent: August 16

I'm sitting here typing this with my maternity bra on with the flaps down with my boobs flapping in the wind. I'm so sore I have to chew on my shirt when I feed him to keep from screaming. Everything I've read says I need to work on the latch some more because it should not hurt this bad.

My sister is going to watch Gage while I get my hair done and go to the dentist. Then I'm having dinner and drinks with some girls from work. Big day for me ... I'm sure I'll freak out and have to come back home to make sure he's okay. At least he'll get bottle fed a few times today and maybe my poor skin can heal a bit.

From: Kim
To: Celeste, Natalie
Sent: August 16

One of the suggestions in the breastfeeding book I read stated that you can try rubbing a few drops of your own milk on your poor boobs and letting it air dry (if they are chapped).

Can you call the lactation consultants at work and ask to come in so they can see his latch? I know they do this where I am delivering with a lot of the patients because many, MANY people needed help with breastfeeding several weeks after delivery. So at least you are not alone in that aspect.

My husband gets quite the show each night when I finally take my bra off as my boobs itch so bad I stand there for a minute scratching them and saying to Ben, "You don't even know ... " I have noticed that if he hears me in the bedroom getting undressed he magically appears to watch this spectacle. It's almost like when the dog is in another part of the house and he hears me open the drawer with his leash and comes running.

From: Celeste
To: Kim, Natalie
Sent: August 20

Let me preface this comment by saying that John was at the appointment when the doctor said, "I have only seen veins this bad, this early in pregnancy, one other time" and "Yes, your hemorrhoid is the size of Mount Everest."

So last night John wants to know if I want some Cold Stone Creamery. In response, I say, "You know what sounds good?" and he says, "Sex?" What?

Is there something wrong with this man? How did we go from ice cream to sex in three seconds?

 From: Kim
To: Celeste, Natalie
Sent: August 20

Ben doesn't even want to touch my boobs for fear of turning me on and it leading to something more. And to answer your question, no, ice cream should not shoot to sex in three seconds. He is either over-sexed or there is something that is misfiring in his brain. I feel for you!

 From: Natalie
To: Kim, Celeste
Sent: August 20

You always want what you can't have.

Did I mention that you girls are looking great. I'm not patronizing or being nice ... seriously you look good.

Gage has had a rough day. He slept okay during the night but has been Sponge Bob Cranky Pants all day. He was inconsolable so we both finally passed out for two hours ... all he wants to do is eat.

Brad was getting really pissy and saying things like, "He is just trying to get attention." I tried to calmly explain that a three-week-old hasn't mastered that art yet and he's probably just growing or something and needs to eat a lot today. I've read that you need to cater to babies to create a safe environment and then you can start cutting back and letting them fuss a bit. Would you agree with this?

From: Kim
To: Celeste, Natalie
Sent: August 21

That is what I have read as well. I think you are also right about the growth spurt. The first year a baby triples its size so this would make sense to me. I think it is a man thing, which is why women are usually the primary caregivers.

Thanks for the compliment. Between my pinched nerve in my back, my groin muscle that continuously hurts, little twinges of pain in the nether regions, and a baby in my lungs, I can't say that I am feeling all that great. For some reason I am now waking up about once every hour or so. When I get up in the morning I feel very drugged and sick.

I have also noticed a lot more Braxton Hicks. I had another baby shower yesterday. Would you believe at this point that I have not received one bottle or breastfeeding item? I did get my first (and only) pack of diapers and wipes last night. I have gotten a lot of big ticket items though so I can't complain.

From: Celeste
To: Natalie, Kim
Sent: August 21

John would always say that kind of stuff too ... hello! All they know is that they are tired, hungry, uncomfortable, or wet! I had people tell me that I needed to start right away with the whole let-them-cry-it-out bit—no snuggling or they will get used to it and be spoiled.

I couldn't do it. I figured I would get tough after she was at least three months old. I wanted her to know that she could count on me for anything and she didn't need to soothe herself if she didn't want to ... we both gradually figured things out and I think she is pretty well adjusted/attached and able to put herself to sleep in her own room, so I am sticking with my plan for the next one.

Delivering the Truth

We know there are many different schools of thought on how to soothe a baby. You will hear lots of advice that has been handed down from generation to generation, like putting whisky on a baby's gums to help with teething or letting a baby cry it out. We do not subscribe to either of these archaic ideas. Co-sleeping with your baby is also a hot topic. If you intend on co-sleeping, please do your research on safe ways to do this.

From: Kim
To: Natalie, Celeste
Sent: August 21

Again, I would agree with Celeste. Everything that I have read states that you are on-call for your baby's needs for the first few months and your child cannot be held or soothed enough during this time.

From: Natalie
To: Celeste, Kim
Sent: August 21

As I type my child is sleeping on his stomach on the couch ... don't call CPS. He sleeps so much better on his stomach. He always wakes up with a snotty nose and I think he has better air flow this way. I keep him in my sight and check on him constantly ... the things we do for sleep, I guess. My back is breaking because I've had to hold him for about thirty straight hours.

I also started pumping today to make sure that I'm getting enough milk out and give my poor boobs a break. We'll see how it goes. At this point I'm a feeding away from supplementing formula ... but I've been here before.

From: Kim
To: Natalie, Celeste
Sent: August 22

So had the big "exam" today. I am 50 percent effaced and fingertip. My translation is that I will be like this forever as

I remember hearing stories of patients who were 80 percent effaced and 3 cm dilated for weeks. However, she asked me if I was having contractions and I said, "No, I have Braxton Hicks all the time but not consistent and they aren't painful."

She says, "Well, if you go into labor this week, make sure you call the office." What? We both know I am not going into labor this week. Or do you know something I don't know? I feel a little paranoid like everyone knows something I don't. I am planning on going past my due date as I have a test on the Sept 25th.

The good news is that her head is down where it is supposed to be and the likelihood of her moving into the butt first position is not favorable. The other good news is that the hospital RNs try to put the baby to breast within twenty minutes after delivering the placenta.

On a funnier note, I told Ben about what John said (the Cold Stone Creamery vs. Sex comment). I then stated that I had told Celeste that Ben had no interest in touching me at this point in time. He got all anxious and said, "She knows why, doesn't she?"

My reply, "Yes, Ben, it has nothing to do with your manlihood and everything to do with the fact that you don't want to harm the baby with your gigantic pecker." He was much relieved.

From: Celeste
To: Kim, Natalie
Sent: August 22

So the exam was not as bad as you thought it would be. I would say that you are going to be preggo for a while now. You will not go into labor until at least next week because we are having that baby shower for you on Sunday, and you better make it there after all the planning we have done!

Maybe you will deliver earlier than your due date, but not within the next two weeks. Did she say how big she thought the baby was?

I am so glad that Ben understands that his manlihood is not in question ... maybe John, Ben, and Brad can all get together and go to a strip club and get this pent-up sexual frustration out of them.

From: Kim
To: Natalie, Celeste
Sent: August 22

We finally finished painting the nursery. My fabulous idea of putting floor to ceiling diamonds on one wall has not turned out as expected. Sure, it always looks great on HGTV but damned if it doesn't look hideous in the baby's room. The problem is, it took us a long time to get the diamonds just right and perfect so I can't justify painting over them.

To top things off, we were putting the crib together last night and one side did not have any holes drilled into it so we couldn't put it together! Not to mention that one of the handles for the drawer was drilled wrong so it can't be screwed in. This was not cheap furniture, people, and we should not be having these problems! They already had to order a new dresser for the boys' room since the drawers were all jacked up when they brought it over! Grrr.

Someone is going to feel my wrath pretty soon here! And wasn't it nice that I had contractions all yesterday evening after being checked? Can you tell that I am irritable?

And trust me, I truly believe that I will not go into labor until one week earlier than my due date at the most. The "exam" was a breeze and much less uncomfortable than the yearly one is. Although I will admit now I feel like I am having menstrual cramps in my back and belly so I could do without that.

I didn't bother to ask her how big the baby was since all the books have said it is a total guessing game on the doctor's part unless you have another ultrasound done. My vote is 6 pounds but then I did somehow gain 4 pounds in two weeks. It must have been the pizza we had at dinner. So much for only gaining one pound at my last appointment. I am still hoping to stay under 40 pounds of weight gain but am now up to 32.

My cousin was nice enough to tell me that you immediately drop 20 pounds after delivery. I like her.

Dr. Bob says

Knowing baby's weight before delivery: how accurate and why do we care? The importance of estimating baby's weight in utero near term is important for a few reasons. (1) to win the baby pool! (2) curiosity, and (3) for physicians to have the information heading into delivery to be aware of potential issues during labor and delivery.

How we estimate nowadays is primarily by ultrasound. However, using Leopold's maneuvers, a method of using the health care provider's hands on the maternal abdomen, is also valid and, in experienced hands, quite reliable. As the pregnancy progresses, our ability to estimate fetal weight regardless of method becomes less accurate. Typically, at term, ultrasound has a +/- 1 percent range of error. In other words, if it is estimated to be 10 pounds, it could be 9 to 11 pounds!

From: Natalie
To: Kim, Celeste
Sent: August 23

This morning I woke up with a temp of 101 and I'm achy all over ... especially in my back and breasts. I need to call the doctor and see what the hell is wrong with me now. I'm teary today—loss of coping strategy right now. I've diagnosed myself with mastitis, a UTI, or a wound infection. I put him in his swing and thank Jesus in heaven he is sleeping right now.

From: Kim
To: Natalie, Celeste
Sent: August 23

Isn't it just one thing after another? Good lord! I hope you feel better!

From: Natalie
To: Kim, Celeste
Sent: August 23

I have mastitis. My temp went up to 103 but has now broken and is 99. I'm on an antibiotic and Motrin. I'm supposed to feed him directly—not pump—which kills me. Good times. My sister spent today with me and let me sleep and took care of Gage. My mom is coming in town tonight to stay with me through the weekend since Brad will be out of town. Hopefully this is it ... and I'll be on the mend.

From: Kim
To: Natalie, Celeste
Sent: August 23

I'm sorry! That sucks!

From: Celeste
To: Kim, Natalie
Sent: August 24

Wow ... that really sucks! I bet you feel like shit. That is all I have heard from people who have had mastitis is that they feel like shit. At least you have your mom and sister to lean on.

From: Natalie
To: Kim, Celeste
Sent: August 24

My fever spiked again last night ... my mom is here and I'm glad about it. She can at least take care of him and I can just feed him and sleep. I feel like I have the flu. It kills me to feed him. Seriously it hurts so bad I can't even explain it. I really want to do formula once the mastitis is gone. I guess it isn't the greatest time to quit but I hope to quit soon.

From: Kim
To: Natalie, Celeste
Sent: August 30

If one more person tells me my pregnancy has gone by fast, I swear to God I will reach out and smack them as hard as I can! The baby is lying on my nerve and the treatment is to get myself on all fours. Hello. When do I have time to sit down and put my feet up let alone sit there on all fours? In addition, I think I have come pretty darn close to peeing my pants on several occasions when she karate chops my bladder.

September

From: Kim
To: Celeste, Natalie
Sent: September 1

Well, I was properly reprimanded by my MD's nurse today. I called because my feet are getting quite swollen and no amount (gallons) of water or putting the pups up is helping. They get swollen enough that my skin is actually quite tight and hurts.

So she is checking into that for me (I hope she will say, "Don't go to work anymore."). Then I asked, "I have a meeting in Lincoln coming up ... is that a big deal?" For God's sake it is only forty-five minutes away. Whoa Nellie! Absolutely not. You should not travel anywhere in the last month of pregnancy. You have no idea what will happen and you don't want to be that far away ... blah, blah, blah.

Good thing I didn't tell her that I actually considered going to the NU game this weekend with you, huh, Celeste? I may have gotten an ass whipping by her! ☺

Natalie, I'm worried though. Haven't heard from you lately! Are you having signs or symptoms of PPD? A psychotic break? Did your mastitis clear up? Is Gage walking now?

Dr. Bob says

Traveling in late pregnancy is a common discussion. The main reason travel is discouraged is due to the chance of delivering while traveling. There is no absolute time to stop traveling. Most health care providers would typically recommend no travel somewhere between thirty-two and thirty-six weeks in an uncomplicated pregnancy.

When traveling, be sure to remember to walk around every few hours and work your calf muscles to prevent blood clots, which sedentary pregnant patients are at increased risk for.

Swelling in pregnancy is quite common in the feet and lower legs anyway. Multiple factors contribute to this including retention of fluids, increased production of fluids, growing uterine size, and potential hormonal changes. It usually goes away after delivery, although some women may have worse swelling for a short period of time after delivery.

To help avoid swelling in pregnancy, you might try getting off your feet, sleep on your sides, wear compression stockings, avoid heat, get daily physical activity, and drink enough water. While mild swelling is normal, if you experience severe, sudden onset of swelling of only one foot or leg, contact your health care provider because this could be a sign of preeclampsia (a potentially serious condition of pregnancy) or a blood clot.

From: Celeste
To: Kim, Natalie
Sent: September 1

Wow that sucks! I hope your blood pressure is fine and this is just the end-of-the-line swelling.

I had to take off my engagement ring and just keep the wedding band on because of my fat fingers. That just happened Wednesday. I feel fortunate that I was able to wear both rings for so long.

Unfortunately, I think I am off to the store to buy some more jeans. I only have one pair that I can wear, and they keep falling down because the elastic waist is so worn out from wearing them 24/7 with Anna. It is always a sad day when you start growing out of your maternity clothes.

From: Kim
To: Natalie, Celeste
Sent: September 1

You didn't grow out of them ... they wore out. Totally not your fault! And remember, ice cream is a dairy product and an essential part of your diet! I've decided I am going past being swollen and have developed elephantiasis.

From: Natalie
To: Celeste, Kim
Sent: September 1

I'm alive. I have a very high needs baby who has to be held and fed constantly ... leaving very limited keyboard time. Right now he's screaming while in the baby snugli. More later.

 From: Natalie
To: Celeste, Kim
Sent: September 2

My sister has been here today so I can actually do something besides hold my kid. YEAH!

I'm trying to wean him ... slowly ... slowly. It's painful. So far I've only been able to go five hours between feedings. And at night? Forget it ... I just feed him from me. It's way quicker.

Have I told you how freaking painful breastfeeding is? Seriously ... couldn't God have invented a spigot of some sort that drains milk from the woman's body? Must it come from the most sensitive part? I need to write a strongly worded letter to him to discuss the matter.

Dear Creator of all things,

First of all, thank you for my son. He's healthy and he arrived here safely. Thank you for healing my body. After a few minor catastrophes, I'm healing up. As the saying goes, "What doesn't kill you makes you stronger." I'm the strongest freaking woman on the planet by now.

Thank you for a sweet husband who is a great dad.

Now, onto the reason for my letter. The breastfeeding thing. I realize you have infinite wisdom and are a master at the grand design of the human body. I also know that we humans are evolving as the years go by. I'm asking you to consider redesigning the breastfeeding mechanism on the newer models. In fact, maybe you could rename the process "knee feeding" or "lower left quadrant" feeding. And there is always my favorite, "left index finger feeding."

The breastfeeding is really a poor design. Frankly, it's downright painful. You've probably gathered that it is rather painful by the number of women who use your name in vain, pray the rosary, or use that time to pray to you ... it takes all of my being not to bite through my tongue or my shirt.

Please take this under consideration. It doesn't have to be an immediate change, but I plan on having another child in a few years so if you could get the plans drawn up and sent to me for approval, we could really push this deal through.

Thanks, God.

Love, your friend,

Natalie

From: Kim
To: Celeste, Natalie
Sent: September 4

Although I found your email and letter to God extremely humorous, I started having these thoughts of, "Oh Dear God ... if Natalie can't tolerate it, am I going to be able to?"

These are not good thoughts to have three weeks before the due date. I am seriously considering pulling out of this game in the ninth inning. There are some days, like today, when I am trying to get all my homework done for the following week, that I want to run outside and scream, "Never mind! I quit! I quit!"

You girls remember in my eighth month (seems so long ago ...) that I was having majorly painful GI issues in which you recommended Colace? You also remember my big plan of working my way up to three a day plus Frosted Mini Wheats at every meal?

Well, I ran out of Colace two weeks ago. Instead of getting backed up, I am totally free flowing now. I swear, where does it all come from? I am having the exact opposite problem now, and I am not even medicating myself! What the hell! The delivery room is not going to be pretty after I am done.

... and the flatulence issue! Dear God in heaven! I used to yell at Ben whenever he let one "slip" as I get so disgusted with the awful noise pollution. But I tell you, I have developed silent killers. I try to hold it until I am alone and inevitably he will walk into the room after I have let one go. Do you know how hard it is to do CPR on someone when you are nine months pregnant?

I will also state that I am officially in mourning. It was difficult to see the zebra stripes appear all over my ass during the eighth month, but I was thankful that they are in a spot that will always be covered by clothing.

It was hard when Ben said to me two weeks ago, "You have a bunch of stretch marks under your boobs now." That was hard because the reality is I am outgrowing my bra (again). These things were hard to take but like a real woman, I took them head on. But damnit! I cannot take the fact that my belly button is popping out! This is sick and wrong!

So my suggestion is that when we are all done with this we send a little bit longer letter to God and ask him to have a nice long chat with Mary about the whole pregnancy situation. If this is payback for Eve eating the apple, then I think we all have paid enough!

From: Kim
To: Celeste, Natalie
Sent: September 4

I am so tired of bowel movements being the central focus of my life. No sooner did I get done sending out my last email than I had to run upstairs for the wonderful experience of what must have been acid shooting out of my rear end. I know this is gross and disgusting, but I am in pain and am feeling really sorry for myself right now.

From: Natalie
To: Celeste, Kim
Sent: September 4

I didn't mean to give the impression that I can't take it. I just thought that after I went through labor and delivery it would be smooth sailing from that point on. We are tough women ... we can take it. I say this as I have cabbage leaves on my boobs trying to quit nursing without getting mastitis again. You could seriously bounce a quarter off my boobs right now. It's not pretty.

As far as your chili ass, Kim ... I wouldn't trust it. How daring you are to run out of Colace and chance it. I'm sure my experience is a total rare thing to happen. I really think your digestive tract shuts down during labor and delivery (for the most part) so you will keep your bodily fluids from shooting out. If not, you will never know. I don't know if I did. Brad doesn't know. So in my mind nothing happened.

Damn ... crying kid again. I'll check in tomorrow.

From: Kim
To: Celeste, Natalie
Sent: September 4

I totally plan on taking Colace the minute I deliver but as of right now, I am going on week two of loose bowels and feel that it would be dangerous to those around me if I started taking it again.

I cannot believe the crap that you have gone through for delivery and breastfeeding. I don't know about Celeste, but I feel like I am almost in the clear because you had just about everything go wrong that could. Whether it is true or not, it definitely makes me feel more comfortable to believe that you definitely took it for the team with your experiences!

By the way, Natalie, when did you lose your mucous plug? I have another MD appt tomorrow. Who wants to bet that I am still just 50 percent effaced? Anyone? Anyone?

From: Natalie
To: Kim, Celeste
Sent: September 5

typing one handed here so please forgive lost plug about 10 days before delivery—I was dilated to 3 & 70% effaced too. did u lose yours?

From: Kim
To: Celeste, Natalie
Sent: September 5

Oh please, girl! No, I imagine I won't lose mine until a week after my due date. Whatever.

I had my MD appt today and am now 70 percent effaced, but still fingertip. My MD and I went back and forth with this conversation:

Her: "You really could go at any time now."

Me: "Riiigghhhtt."

Her: "No, seriously, it could be any day now."

Me: "Mhmmm."

I am finally uncomfortable at night now. Furthermore, Ben and I switched sides so I can get out of bed easier. He isn't adjusting too well. The other night his hand flew in my face about four times and he kept trying to roll back to his side and steal my body pillow.

Last night was a bit of improvement as I only got a hand in my face once, which I promptly picked up and threw back over toward his side of the bed. I learned this morning that it did stay attached to his body.

 From: Celeste
To: Kim, Natalie
Sent: September 5

I am having sleeping issues too ...

I don't ever remember having sleeping issues while pregnant with Anna, but now I can't lie down on my back without getting short of breath. I always have to have my head elevated, which defeats the purpose of having my bottom half above my heart to decrease the pressure in the lower region and decrease the varicose veins.

I really feel like I would be most comfortable if I were sitting in the lazy-boy all day long and then just sleeping there. So basically, I would like to sit all day and not move.

I am also having boob issues. Can either one of you explain to me how it is that I do not have a child breastfeeding on my already sore boobs and still have six weeks of torturous pregnancy to endure, and I already have a cracked nipple? What is this about? I am quite positive that if a kid actually uses the nipple to get nourishment, then the nipple will actually crack completely in half and fall off my body.

I, like Natalie, would not trust the chili ass situation. Ever heard the saying, "This too shall pass?" And once it does pass, you are going to be in a world of hurt if you are not prepared! I would continue to eat the bran every morning and make sure there is Colace around for the one day you actually skip the lovely trip to the bathroom ... because if you are anything like me, you forget about it for one day and that day turns into four and then you are like Natalie and biting through towels and chipping your teeth.

I spent $175 at Target today. I bought my first package of newborn diapers and a package of unisex bag sleepers. I realized that I gave away all of my unisex sleepers to one of Natalie's friends when she became pregnant with twins. I also bought a few new nipples for my Avent bottles. I think I am starting to nest.

 From: Kim
To: Celeste, Natalie
Sent: September 5

Ooh ... a cracked nipple already? Maybe you are having signs of sympathy boobs for Natalie? Two nights ago I was studying at the table and I looked down and saw a wet spot on my shirt right were my boob is. There were no liquids anywhere near me at all.

Ben saw it too so I know I wasn't hallucinating. I have convinced myself it had a more "chemical" smell and therefore could not be anything biohazardous in nature.

You girls do not seem to understand the situation here ... we are not talking your basic loose stools. We are talking about liquid fire coming out of my ass for the past few days. If I were to take Colace or eat my traditional Mini Wheats, well, who knows what would happen! I do promise that the minute I firm up I will again eat my Mini Wheats and have Colace on hand.

I am a bit confused. You bought a bag of diapers and some sleep sacks and spent $175? ☺ I think you should just sleep on the lazy-boy. They say we aren't supposed to be on our backs and stay on our left sides but tell me this, who told the cave woman about this and every other woman after her who did just fine in her pregnancy? I don't know how this will address your vein problem but am assuming if you can breathe, that is a good thing in itself.

Dr. Bob says

In the first and early second trimester, whatever position is most comfortable for sleeping is fine. However, in the later second and third trimester, it is recommended to avoid sleeping on your back. This is to avoid compression of the vena cava (the main blood vessel returning blood to your heart).

So the recommendation is to sleep on your sides or at least tilted off your back. Use pillows or whatever it takes. If you wake up on your back, don't wig out. Just go to the bathroom (again) if needed and try to get comfortable (again) off your back. If you do wake up on your back or belly, it will not harm your baby or you. The fact you woke up is probably your body's way to let you know to change positions.

From: Natalie
To: Celeste, Kim
Sent: September 5

This will have to be quick because my child has only slept fifteen minutes since 9 a.m. I have done nothing but hold, rock, and feed this monster. He is finally down in his bassinet but wiggling around and making noise. WTH??

Brad is leaving for Florida tomorrow and won't be back until Monday. I'm not thrilled.

Cracked nipples already? Celeste, I do remember you telling me that your boobs started to leak very early in your pregnancy with Anna. Repeat performance?

Chili ass—I don't trust it. At least you know what to do when the time comes. Bad deal. As far as the "any day now" comment from your MD—I really wish they would not say that. My doctor said that to me and the next morning I lost the plug and then sat for another ten days—which seemed like ETERNITY.

I tell you—raw cabbage leaves are IT! I have only been feeding him a few minutes two or three times a day. Yesterday I thought my boobs would split open and leak all over the place (actually I did leak when he was crying last night—that was a first). But I went and bought cabbage leaves and have been putting them on every two hours. And today my boobs are hard but not like yesterday and I can nearly stand to hold him next to me (handy for today).

I guess he must be growing today with all the crying and eating. It's a very weird feeling to love someone so much and want to bounce them against the wall at the same time. No worries girls ... I'd never do it.

Maybe he'll sleep all night tonight ... HAHAHAHAHAHAHA

Delivering the Truth

There will be times when you feel like nothing you are doing is calming your child. This is a normal part of parenthood. Know when you have reached your limit. Put the baby in a safe place (a crib or baby swing, for example) and take a few minutes for yourself. All they know is that in their little world, they have a need and cannot meet that need themselves. Above all, *never* shake a baby.

From: Celeste
To: Natalie, Kim
Sent: September 6

So, have you tried Haagen Dazs fat free lemon sorbet? I am addicted.

From: Kim
To: Celeste, Natalie
Sent: September 6

Fat free is not in my vocabulary right now.

 From: Celeste
To: Natalie, Kim
Sent: September 6

Do you think it is normal to have what I can only describe as pelvic bone pain?

It isn't in my butt, but down below, but it feels like it is inside, not exterior like my veins.

What could this be? Please tell me it doesn't warrant a call to the nurse, who already knows I am a freak.

And the feeling of loving this child so much and wanting to throw them against the wall doesn't go away after they are two. Maybe it goes away after they are eighteen.

 From: Kim
To: Celeste, Natalie
Sent: September 6

I can't really comment if your pelvic pain is normal in this stage of the game. I know that I have it now, plus all sorts of other twinges and shooting pains going on in that general region. I am assuming it is normal. Natalie? What say you?

From: Natalie
To: Kim, Celeste
Sent: September 6

I have a minute of sleeping bliss so I'll type fast. Brad is in Florida for softball. It's a really fun tourney. I went last year and had a blast. I'm very sad, and pissed, that he is gone. But what is the alternative? Pack up the kid and get my jelly-filled body into a swimsuit and go with? No. This is an annual trip. I knew it was coming.

Pelvic pain. I had pain on the inside of my thigh—like groin pain. It was worse than my hip pain. I asked my doctor about it. He said it is muscle pain. Basically your hip is going out of joint to make room for the alien to come out. Maybe you should have a strong discussion with your fetus and tell him/her that is not the exit he/she has been assigned to.

Last night I was feeding him (from me) and he again had blood coming out of his mouth. I bled through my bra. It's a cracked nipple. But when I tried to pump MINIMAL comes out. I can feel my boob is hard and lumpy but nothing comes out. I hope nothing is blocked. I have been putting so many cabbage leaves on myself I reek.

Okay, gotta wake him up (it nearly kills me to do so), shove some food down his gullet and head to the MD. I hope he won't cry his head off.

From: Kim
To: Natalie, Celeste
Sent: September 6

Hmmm ... Good to know about the muscle pain.

Have you talked to a lactation consultant at all? I have to believe that life could be a little better for you (because this makes me feel better in the long run!). I know you and Celeste are weirded out by this, but I love the gals at my hospital and they would be more than happy to take your call especially if you said their favorite social worker (... uhm ... that would be me in case you were wondering!) told you to call. There has got to be something that makes you hurt less (or at least lie to me about it—ha!).

I still say you get the Mom of the Year award, and as soon as you are mentally/physically ready, you are entitled to a weekend vacation somewhere by yourself!

 From: Celeste
To: Kim, Natalie
Sent: September 6

My boob itches. I have used Lansinoh cream on it to help with the chapped and cracked areas, but it itches all the flippen' time! I have not changed detergents or anything, so I can't figure out what is going on. Of course, I have diagnosed my boob with either a yeast infection or some other funky thing that will get into my boob and cause either mastitis or horrible milk that my kid can't eat.

As for the pelvic pain, I thought it was probably my pelvis getting soft and stretching apart to allow for the baby to slide right on through. I have not had the much needed conversation with Little Fetus to discuss the proper exiting technique. I will discuss that with him/her tonight after Anna goes to bed.

I am all for leaving all kids with husbands and going on vacation with other women who have funky bodies after having children. I am used to the whole "I gotta be out of town for four days" bit because of John's traveling for work. As much as I understand the need to be gone, after about three weeks of seeing him on the weekend in between golf games, I start to go crazy and get resentful when he acts annoyed that I am going to dinner with a friend.

This is an ongoing discussion with us. I don't know if he is getting better about it or if I am getting used to the schedule, but things seem better right now. Wait until I have this baby, then I will be a total freak again and flip out when he tells me he wants to go play golf.

From: Kim
To: Celeste, Natalie
Sent: September 6

I am sure that my boobs don't itch as bad as yours, but I think I did email you before about how if Ben hears me getting undressed he comes into the room because he knows I am going to sit there for the next five minutes and scratch the girls.

We are providing a safe environment here. You can talk about bouncing your child against a wall and we know that you would never do it but just saying it may help a little.

This child has got to get off my nerve. There are some moments where I am fine and other moments when I can barely walk ... literally. Last night I got out of bed to use the bathroom ... for the umpteenth time ... and about screamed in agony. Thank God I only have three weeks left.

Brad is going to Florida? You are a bigger person than I am. I plan to make Ben a slave to the house until I state otherwise ... which will probably be at least eighteen years or so by my guestimation.

From: Natalie
To: Celeste, Kim
Sent: September 8

I am being punked. That is the only explanation. I went to the Urgent Care last night with a high fever again. I now have pyelonephritis (kidney infection), mastitis (again), and thrush on my nipples (which means Gage has it in his mouth).

I'm so f***ing pissed.

 From: Kim
To: Celeste, Natalie
Sent: September 8

The gods must be against you. This is the only explanation. How unfair. How much more can a woman take? Is it time for any psychotropic meds yet? You deserve some heavy narcotics to go to a happy place for a little while. On the flip side, won't Gage look so cute with a blue mouth and your matching blue nipples? Be sure to take pictures!

From: Natalie
To: Celeste, Kim
Sent: September 8

Gage is not going anywhere near my nipples. I'm totally engorged and it hurts like hell, but I don't care. Breast milk be gone! I nearly started crying at the Urgent Care last night. Just a little overwhelmed. My sister is here since I cannot stand to hold him against my chest. Is this my punishment for a relatively easy pregnancy?

The lactation lady at the hospital said stick with the cabbage leaves, ice packs, and don't pump—and it should subside in a few days (AHHHHH!). It's already been a few days. I go for my six-week check on Tuesday. I might have a breakdown and end up with a social work consult. At this point I'm ready for a mastectomy.

From: Celeste
To: Kim, Natalie
Sent: September 8

I agree 100 percent that you are being punked.

And a mastectomy sounds like a reasonable option at this point. I can't believe all the shit that is rolling your way. It definitely makes me fearful of what is to come. I had it relatively easy with Anna after she was born. Will I get paybacks too? I wonder if I will be doomed with a two-year-old who doesn't adjust and a newborn with colic.

You have every right in the world to be pissed—at everyone. Thank God for your sister and for antibiotics. When do you get to drink a nice big beer and not be responsible for your actions if you get drunk?

From: Kim
To: Celeste, Natalie
Sent: September 8

All I have to say is that I won't be able to take any of the crap that has happened to Natalie and still try to attend two classes.

My new mantra, "It only happens to Natalie ... It only happens to Natalie ... " This sounds much like Dorothy saying, "There is no place like home ... "

I believe right about now both of you are supposed to be blowing a whole bunch of smoke up my ass with how great the whole delivery will be since I am due in a little over two weeks. You're not playing fair here.

From: Natalie
To: Celeste, Kim
Sent: September 9

Yes, it's to the point where I don't even want to tell you girls because you'll think I'm making it up. I wish I was making it up.

I'm better today. Antibiotics on board and the purple nipple stuff and I'm nearly a new woman.

I fear I have a problem in the nether regions where things ripped. It still bleeds. I took a mirror and checked the damage. There is still some damage. It looks as though it could use some stitches. YIKES. I guess we'll see what the doctor says on Tuesday.

You girls will sail through your deliveries! You will not have trouble breastfeeding or stopping when you are ready. You will heal perfectly back together and be in your skinny jeans in two weeks. I just know it.

Please don't let my woes skew your view. Kim, you're on deck. You are next. It will be the best day of your life. I'm not going to fill you with cheesy things—but seriously—it was such an exciting day for me. I've never felt closer to Brad—and there are simply no words to describe the feeling of having your baby placed on you for the first time. It will be spectacular. I would do it again tomorrow—all things considered. THIS IS NOT BLOWING SMOKE, KIM!

And if there are a few bumps in the road post delivery, you will deal with them. You have good friends and family that will help you wherever you need it. You will graduate. Don't fret.

When will I be able to wear my regular clothes again? I can get my pants on and zipped but then I have a huge roll—and let me tell you how attractive it looks when I put a shirt on over it. Wow! Look out, ladies! Hold on to your men! I'm one hot ticket.

From: Kim
To: Celeste, Natalie
Sent: September 12

Here is my status: 1 cm and still 70 percent effaced. No snot in my underwear yet either.

From: Celeste
To: Kim, Natalie
Sent: September 12

Well, Kim, at least it looks like you might make it to your test on September 25th.

A friend of mine had a baby and he was born with a heart condition and will have to have open heart surgery. How did they not know this on ultrasound? I flipped out today on my doctor about this, and he said it is difficult to see on ultrasound but there are usually small indicators.

Then as I was getting ready to go, he says, "Okay, see you in two weeks and if you want, we can look at the heart and make sure everything is okay."

God bless him.

From: Kim
To: Celeste, Natalie
Sent: September 12

A girl at work thinks I will deliver on the 17th. She just has a "feeling." Everyone keeps asking me if I am excited. Uhm ... no ... I have no idea what to expect and I know the crazy amount of work that is coming once she is here, so quit asking me if I am excited.

I would also like to lodge a complaint with whoever is responsible for wanting my urine sample each week. Do they really think I can see where I am peeing due to my oversized belly? How the hell do I aim for the cup when I can't see it?

From: Natalie
To: Celeste, Kim
Sent: September 13

Just wait until you nearly kill someone for peeking into your office and saying, "You're STILL here??" Or saying helpful things like, "She'll come when she's ready" ... WHAT ABOUT ME ... I'M READY NOW!

I won't try to butter you up with catchy phrases.

Had my six-week check. She had to use silver nitrate sticks to um ... cauterize ... something. It hurt, but what is the alternative? She said, "Can your husband hold off for another two weeks??" I told her we had already decided to just be friends. The exam was painful ... I can't imagine sex.

Brad didn't get home until 8 p.m. last night so my plans for a fun family night were shot. I want to start going to the gym but he needs to be home and available to take care of the kiddo for a while. This gut, hips, thighs, and double chin have got to go. They have worn out their welcome.

Kim, try another cheer. It just might work. Oh, one piece of advice that I actually did was from the midwife at work. She said get in the tub and squat and bear down as hard as you can and then do nipple stimulation for as long as you can stand it each night. I was willing to drink castor oil, so this was a less disgusting alternative.

From: Kim
To: Celeste, Natalie
Sent: September 13

I can honestly say at this point that I am not ready to have her. I am not terribly uncomfortable ... yet. My MD said I can sit in our hot tub if it is below 100 (so, of course, we keep it at 98). I do this every night and it helps me go to sleep.

I also have only been getting up two times a night as opposed to four so I am not complaining at all.

My teacher assigned a mini-paper that is due on my due date. So I am thinking if she can wait until I am done with my test, turn in that paper, and turn in my scholarship applications, that would be just great. I would really like to deliver on the 30th so

I can also go to a conference for work, but I won't push it. I will keep your advice in mind though, if I change my mind.

Exactly why was the exam painful? Other than getting cauterized of course. Was there some basic exam thing she did that hurt or was it all related to your other issue? I cancelled my gym membership, which made me sad but I refuse to pay $40 a month when I have not been able to go since I started school. I have no idea how I will shrink back after this baby comes. I am worried because I am so much wider now that I will not fit back into my other clothes simply because my body has permanently changed in shape.

How weird to think that you (Celeste) are going to be delivering a baby about two weeks after me!

Dr. Bob says

You should avoid excessive heat in pregnancy that could raise your core body temperature to 102 F or 38.9 C. Typical things that can do this are hot tubs, saunas, electric blankets or heating pads, becoming overheated outside, fevers, or potentially hot, hot showers or baths. The reason is that if the core body temperature is 102 or above, it can result in problems for the baby including birth defects, depending on when in the pregnancy it occurs.

From: Natalie
To: Celeste, Kim
Sent: September 13

Well, then it's official. You'll go early. However, maybe she is a well-behaved baby and will listen to your wishes. You guys have a hot tub? I'm jealous. We keep talking about getting one, but always find other things to spend the cash on. That is great that it helps you sleep.

The exam was painful because ... she did a full exam (Pap and all) and it just hurt. The whole speculum thingy. Now I'm worried about what is the next step if this cauterization doesn't work. Then what? I'm sure it's just painful because the southern hemisphere of my body has been off limits for quite a while.

I'm wider too. My pants go on but don't close. My shirts go on but don't close. It's a joy.

From: Kim
To: Celeste, Natalie
Sent: September 14

Dang! I was hoping you would be able to say, "It's a miracle! My body has gone back to the size it was before I delivered!" I don't want to have to buy a new wardrobe just because my hips have gotten about five inches wider on each side.

From: Natalie
To: Celeste, Kim
Sent: September 14

It's a sad state of affairs when I actually WANT to go to the gym but can't because Brad gets home at 8 p.m. and does computer work, eats and goes to bed before his next fifteen-hour day. Gage can't go to daycare at the gym (which is probably gross anyway) until he's three or six (I can't remember) months old. There is always the walking outside, but it's limited due to feeding issues. I guess there is always plastic surgery.

I'm packing up my maternity clothes though. I kept a few t-shirts out that I wore at the beginning but otherwise it's going into storage. Maybe I'll break out my workout DVDs.

 From: Celeste
To: Kim, Natalie
Sent: September 14

Why did I get pregnant again? Why did I think that I could handle two children?

I can't even handle one child, plus housework, plus laundry, plus the dogs, plus work, plus my crafty crap. I think Anna needs to go to daycare fulltime and then maybe I could get all of my stuff done ... but then I would feel guilty.

Other mothers must be able to do this. Why can't I?

And what in God's name am I going to get done once the baby is born? I am not going to be able to do anything but feed the baby and take care of Anna. I don't think I will even be able to grocery shop.

I think it is time to reevaluate this decision and turn back time.

From: Kim
To: Celeste, Natalie
Sent: September 14

Why must you send me into panic mode? I am fretting about how I am going to get through this semester and keep my sanity ... let alone all the other stuff. I think there is a very slight possibility that I may be slowly losing my mucous plug. God, I hope not—not yet anyway!

From: Natalie
To: Celeste, Kim
Sent: September 15

I don't know how other people do it. Now that Gage is on formula fulltime, I feel like I might actually be able to venture more than a ten-mile radius from home because if all else fails I can give him a bottle.

This is the hardest thing I've ever done. I thought it would totally be a breeze. How much work can a newborn be?

Celeste, you are going to get through this by asking your friends and family for help. You are going to keep your sanity by getting babysitters. If you girls are like me (and I have a sneaking suspicion you are), you will tell everyone that you don't need help and all is well until you have to call your mom crying because your boobs hurt.

I am certainly open to watching babies while moms nap. My sister did that for me and it was a beautiful thing. If Anna has to spend a little more time at daycare for a while, so be it. She will enjoy the socialization and you will enjoy your sanity.

Kim, the plug. It's a bad deal. I'm serious. She's coming a bit early. That is my prediction.

My doctor asked me at my six-week check if I wanted anything for birth control. ARE YOU CRAZY WOMAN? GIVE ME ALL YOU GOT! But it doesn't really matter because Brad and I are just friends.

Also, my house was dangerously close to a CPS investigation. I haven't cleaned it since before Gage was born. I guess I vacuumed once. It's still gross but less gross than before. I think Celeste has the right idea with hiring a cleaning lady.

I think I'd pay top dollar for someone to scrub my tub and shower. I can't bring myself to do it.

From: Kim
To: Celeste, Natalie
Sent: September 15

Too funny! I think you (Celeste) should consider putting Anna in daycare fulltime for the first few months. It may help with the whole sanity thing in the event that your doctor doesn't prescribe you any psychotropic meds.

Seriously, Natalie, why start cleaning your house now? Maybe we should all have a contest to see how long we can let our houses go before someone calls CPS on one of us.

I haven't had any "snot in my underwear" type issues since the very minuscule amount yesterday so I am still holding on for September 30th.

It is a good thing that health care providers don't ask moms if they want to be sterilized at the six-week follow-up.

From: Kim
To: Celeste, Natalie
Sent: September 17

It is starting to get really tough doing this pregnancy thing. My feet swelled up horribly, and they hurt really badly today. I can't get my ring off either.

From: Kim
To: Celeste, Natalie
Sent: September 18

I cannot tell you how much pain I am starting to feel. I wished I could say that at least it was labor pains, but it is more like she is waaayyyy too big for the thin membrane she is encased in and is trying to break it ... that and the occasional feeling that she is sticking her hand through my cervix is quite enjoyable. The one thing that is making this survivable is that I have less than two weeks left.

From: Celeste
To: Kim, Natalie
Sent: September 18

I felt like shit yesterday morning until about 1:30. I was having contractions and cramps and actually went to the bathroom twice! This is amazing since I hardly go once a day ... TMI, I know.

Anyway, Kim, I don't know how you can feel in control. I feel completely out of control. I feel like I have a million things to do and no time to do it. I need to get some work stuff done today and then maybe I will feel better.

I remember getting this way with Anna, only I was freaking out much earlier with her. Now I am a bit psychotic that I don't have things done and ready. I need to go to Babies R Us and get a new monitor, I need to get a new stroller, I need to get more nipples for my bottles, I need diapers (I have one box), I need to finish work stuff and make sure people don't have much to do for me while I am gone, I need to call all of my forty-five families and let them know my schedule for being gone, I need to schedule three more post-placement visits before I leave and do those reports, and I am starting another home study this week.

And this stupid hemorrhoid needs to go! I can barely do anything without my ass screaming at me. Medicine doesn't help. I am afraid it needs to be surgically removed and I don't see my doctor again until next week.

Again I ask myself, why did I think I could handle this??

Oh, and John told me this week that he will be out of town (working) the entire second week this new child is alive. He seems to think that by the time the child is two weeks old, I should be able to handle it. I hope you (Nat) are still off work at that time, cuz it is going to be "gather at Celeste's house to help keep her sanity" week.

Delivering the Truth

Let's face it. The last inning of your pregnancy can be rough. Let's count the ways:

1. Mentally, you are gearing up for delivery at any moment! Consider yourself on *high alert*—<u>Defcon 5</u>!

2. Your maternity clothes no longer fit.

3. Your patience with every human being on the planet is limited. You are surrounded by idiots.

4. You can't eat, move, or sleep well.

On a positive note...

You do have the waddling thing down.

From: Kim
To: Celeste, Natalie
Sent: September 18

Hmm ... I can see why you are stressed as this seemed to be my mode last week. However, I got one thing done ... then another and then another and now I feel in control.

Perhaps start with the trip to Babies R Us since I have coupons for some of your bigger ticket items (like $25 off). Let me know if you want them or not. I have only two packages of the newborn diapers because I didn't want to buy more and have her grow out of them too fast. The MD feels pretty confident that I am having around a seven pounder so I guess I should go buy some more?

I wanted to get our carpets cleaned before she arrives because we haven't had it done in almost a year and I think the house stinks. Ben said he thought he heard someone say that you shouldn't have your carpets cleaned before you bring a baby home because you stir up all the allergens and crap. Have you heard this?

I almost fell off the chair last night because I had the most horribly excruciating pain radiate down my leg (from the nerve that constantly hurts anyway). I got up and almost couldn't walk—seriously. It is better today but it is a good thing I don't have much longer because walking like an old lady does not suit my style.

From: Natalie
To: Kim, Celeste
Sent: September 18

I only have a minute since the kidlet is passed out in the swing and it's my golden opportunity for a shower. I will do whatever I can to help you girls out.

Celeste, can your mom stay with you while John is gone? Maybe it's a good idea to farm Anna out to friends for the babysitting and put her in daycare fulltime. I seriously think you may snap if you don't.

What is John thinking? You are going to have a c-section to deal with, plus a two-and-a-half-year-old and a newborn. WTH!

Kim, you are feeling shitty because it's the only way you will accept labor and delivery. If you felt fine you would want to be pregnant forever. Feeling like shit gets you in the mindset to get this kid out of you! Serve her the eviction notice (thirty days, remember) and get to movin'!

From: Celeste
To: Natalie, Kim
Sent: September 18

Yea, I am all for sending Anna to daycare fulltime for a while, but (this shows you my stress level) then I freak out about "but how am I actually going to get her to daycare?!" Last time it seemed like I wasn't allowed to drive for a million years, and what if John leaves before I can drive? Can you see the meltdown occurring right before your eyes?

The bug spray people are here, and the guy is very nice. At least I don't have to chop him up into tiny pieces and bury him in the yard. I don't have time for that right now!

From: Kim
To: Celeste, Natalie
Sent: September 18

Well, keep in mind that Jennifer, your very best friend, is coming to town to help you with Anna and the baby. That may give you enough time to get your total meltdown out of the way and then start figuring out how you will do everything.

From: Natalie
To: Celeste, Kim
Sent: September 18

I'm at a loss here. You girls helped me through my meltdowns and I feel as though I'm not helping you through yours. Jennifer will be here to help you, Celeste. You have your mom, you have lots of other friends that can lend a hand. I am happy to help as much as I can without driving you nuts.

From: Celeste
To: Natalie, Kim
Sent: September 18

Do you think that if I have a second helping of the crab salad I made for lunch that I will poison my kid with too much mercury?

From: Kim
To: Celeste, Natalie
Sent: September 18

Nahhhh ... there's probably more mercury in your teeth from fillings when you were younger. Just don't add any swordfish.

Dr. Bob says

Seafood and shellfish can be a very healthy and important part of a pregnancy diet as they contain omega-3 fatty acids and are high in protein and low in saturated fat. Most recommend about 12 ounces a week of fish or shellfish. However, certain fish contain mercury, so avoid them. Fish high in mercury are shark, swordfish, king mackerel, tilefish, and tuna steak. Also, raw or undercooked fish (sushi) and shellfish should be avoided.

From: Kim
To: Celeste, Natalie
Sent: September 18

All of a sudden this past week I am continuously dying of hunger. I cannot get enough to eat. It is almost like the beginning of my pregnancy. I am going to tell myself that it is my body gearing up for the marathon.

From: Natalie
To: Celeste, Kim
Sent: September 18

Maybe? I felt like I didn't have any more room for food (not that it stopped me from eating). Maybe you are carb loading for the marathon.

Can I tell you that Gage is asleep in his CRIB right now—sound the alarm, mark your calendar—HOLY CRAP! Of course I have to go in there every three minutes to make sure he's still breathing.

From: Kim
To: Celeste, Natalie
Sent: September 19

1 cm (still) and 90 percent effaced. The silly woman asked me if I wanted my membranes stripped. Umm no! Keep your hands away from me!

And I just gave Ben the MD update. He asked why I didn't get my membranes stripped if it was an option. Well, for one, it doesn't feel good and two if you want me to go into labor then we can either start having sex again or you can play with my boobs. He says, "What? That's all you have to do?" And meanwhile I am thinking, "What? I might finally get some action?"

From: Natalie
To: Celeste, Kim
Sent: September 19

I was all for the stripping of the membranes ... it wasn't too bad actually. It just didn't hurry things along any.

We are going to try different formula with Gage. I think the Enfamil with Lipil isn't agreeing with him. He seems like his stomach hurts. They have a gentle formula that I'm going to try. I hope that will do it and it's not an allergy of any sort.

Kim, you are a brave woman carrying on with pregnancy. God love ya.

 From: Natalie
To: Celeste, Kim
Sent: September 20

We switched Gage's formula from Enfamil Iron with Lipil to Enfamil GentleEase (for gassy or fussy babies). He woke up at 1 a.m. and ate 2 oz—went right back to sleep. Then he got up at 5 a.m. and ate 4 oz—then up at 7 a.m. and ate 2 oz and went to sleep. THIS IS AMAZING!

Now I may be getting ahead of myself because he was up a lot yesterday crying and fussing, so maybe he's just passed out, but I'm keeping my fingers crossed.

So far, this is a new kid and I'm liking it.

From: Celeste
To: Kim, Natalie
Sent: September 20

Congratulations! That is very exciting and I hope that it isn't a fluke. Maybe this is the start of a schedule and some well-deserved sleep for you!

I am crossing my fingers.

From: Natalie
To: Celeste, Kim
Sent: September 20

I hope so ... so far so good. He was eating about 35 oz a day, which is ALOT so with this formula he can actually wait longer in between feeds and is eating more like 25 oz a day. I think he was just so fussy I kept ramming food down his throat, which he gladly took. Now he naps in between feeds and his head doesn't turn bright red and look like he's going to stroke because his stomach hurts so bad. JEEZ!

From: Kim
To: Celeste, Natalie
Sent: September 20

I am really glad that he might be starting a reasonable schedule! I hope you are getting some extra sleep now.

I think I am slowly losing my mucous plug. It isn't like Natalie's experience though. I have clear slime every day. Nice huh? I had a few contractions that woke me up last night because they were uncomfortable. In addition, my snoring husband and a very wet German Shepherd's nose in my face on three occasions also kept me up. I am extremely tired but need to study for my research test tonight. Ugh.

Ahhh ... another nice contraction. I swear to God if I go another two weeks with this crap I will scream. Shit or get off the pot here!

From: Natalie
To: Celeste, Kim
Sent: September 21

We are going to Kansas City either tonight or tomorrow for the weekend. I swear I'm packing the entire nursery to go with us. I really don't want to go, but I'm being a good wife and going. I'm sure it will be too cold and he'll be too fussy and I'll end up in the hotel room most of the time but oh well. (It's for a softball tourney, of course.)

The formula is still going well. He still seems like he strains a bit but not like before. He's sleeping great at night—eats and goes right back to sleep. He's awake a lot during the day, which I must admit kind of sucks.

From: Kim
To: Celeste, Natalie
Sent: September 21

Good luck on the Kansas City trip! My friend took her baby to the Nebraska game last weekend in California and they seemed to manage ... I hope Gage will be somewhat manageable for you. And you can just pass him around to all of your softball friends to dote on so you get a little bit of a break!

From: Kim
To: Natalie, Celeste
Sent: September 24

Is Jamie getting induced tomorrow? My contractions stopped completely as of Friday. I stopped doing my internship, so now I will work half days Wed thru Fri. I may have her strip my membranes on Friday to see what happens ... if nothing then maybe induce on the following Monday? Not looking forward to either but also don't want to go too long past my due date.

It is amazing the little amount of room that is NOT left and how uncomfortable I am. I can tell that she is totally squished anytime I sit. My stomach is so tight it is now difficult to tell by touch if I am contracting. Have to rely on the feeling on the inside as opposed to the outside.

Did I tell you gals I am now up to three Colace a day? I don't know which I liked better ... chili ass or ...

From: Natalie
To: Celeste, Kim
Sent: September 25

I've been gone since Thursday, any news? If not, I'm sorry for being one of those annoying people that ask.

First out-of-town trip with a baby. WOW! What an experience. He did great. Two of the nights we even had four adults, Gage, and a five-month-old in the same room. (IT SUCKED) but the babies were good.

From: Kim
To: Celeste, Natalie
Sent: September 25

Yes! I am still here. Yes! I am back today. If you see my physical body then one could conclude that I am present and you are not hallucinating. Do not call me daily or email me and ask, "How I'm feeling." I'm feeling like a term pregnant woman— highly irritable with a research methods test to take. Were you people born annoying or is this something that you work at daily to drive me over the edge?

From: Celeste
To: Kim, Natalie
Sent: September 25

Hehehehehehehehe. Gotta love that stage. ☺ I hope you don't kill any poor unsuspecting soul who walks into your office today, but I would back you and testify to temporary insanity.

From: Natalie
To: Celeste, Kim
Sent: September 25

I'll give you the advice you gave me. Put a sign on your office door that says, "Yes, I'm still here so quit asking."

Soon, dear girl ... very soon.

From: Natalie
To: Celeste, Kim
Sent: September 25

Isn't today the big day for Jamie? Who wants to guess what she's having? I guess girl.

Kim, so you ready to talk induction? I was and then I didn't have to, which is good because (1) I dreaded the thought of induction and (2) they told me they would let me go two weeks over—those heartless assholes.

Colace and Milk of Mag—the loves of my life. I still take three Colace a day. I go back AGAIN to the doc (eight-week check) to see if everything is healing. If not, I have no idea what is the next step. Amputation? Can they amputate my vagina?

Contraction Action—What's your reaction?

Push it out, push it out, WAY out!

That's my cheer for today.

From: Celeste
To: Kim, Natalie
Sent: September 25

I kept dreaming about Jamie, and she called me to tell me she had the baby and I asked her what it was and she said "green" as in not pink (girl), not blue (boy), but green—ambiguous genitalia. I think my doctor needs to do another ultrasound just to check and make sure and not tell me the sex, just tell me it is for sure one or the other. And I am going to be a freakish worrier until Jamie or her husband calls me today.

I think I would go for getting the membranes stripped before I go for the full-on induction.

Traveling with a baby sucks. I am glad you made it—and with four adults in one hotel room? NOT fun.

Dr. Bob says

Ambiguous genitalia is a birth defect in which the external or outer genitals do not have the typical appearance of either a boy or a girl. If you are concerned, talk with your health care provider.

From: Natalie
To: Celeste, Kim
Sent: September 25

Your baby is not ambiguous. Really? How rare is that? 1 in 80 zillion?

I think I'm going to take money out of my 401K and work with a trainer at the gym four days a week. I think it would be worth it to get rid of this disgusting roll around my waist. It makes me vomit and want to never eat again. The problem is I hate to vomit and I like food very much. The next thing would be finding time to get to the trainer. I haven't been able to get to the gym yet. I've been running the stairs in my house (like with laundry and take only a few items downstairs and make lots of trips) and doing situps. I need professional trainer help. Maybe if I went at eleven at night when everyone was asleep ... hmmm ...

From: Kim
To: Celeste, Natalie
Sent: September 25

I am going to say boy for Jamie. I am willing to go one week over my due date (which is tomorrow, I might remind everyone) but not two weeks. I just don't feel comfortable going two weeks with a placenta deteriorating and all that.

I don't feel ready for my research test today ... this sucks.

Dr. Bob says

Deteriorating placenta or maturing placenta are vague, slang terms used in reference to the placenta (or afterbirth) in regard to its ability to optimally support the baby in utero. The placenta functions as the life support system for the baby while in the uterus. It is the coolest organ system in humans when you consider what it does!

Over the last two or three decades much attention has been given to placental function using ultrasound. Placental grade was a system used for a period of time, and to a certain degree is still used, although most experts would say that term should not have significance placed on it. It seems that these vague slang references have been derived from this.

Ultimately, if the placenta is not functioning at its optimal ability, it is termed utero-placental insufficiency. There is a multitude of causes for this. Ultimately, in some settings it can result in growth disturbances of the baby, decreased amniotic fluid (water around the baby), or even rarely an increased risk for stillbirth. Your health care provider will monitor for evidence of any of these things and, if concerns arise, will monitor the pregnancy more closely.

From: Celeste
To: Kim, Natalie
Sent: September 25

Heard from Jamie ... It's a GIRL!
They are both doing great!

From: Kim
To: Celeste, Natalie
Sent: September 25

You mean we actually have a baby after we deliver? I thought you just stayed pregnant, went into labor, and that was it.

From: Natalie
To: Celeste, Kim
Sent: September 25

YAHOO!

See? Another woman lives to tell the tale. I'm glad she is doing well. I thought that too, Kim. Then the FUN really begins. You get to heal, go crazy, want to kill your family, cry, AND take care of another human who is totally dependent on you and you have no idea what the hell you are doing. It's great. BIG FUN!

From: Celeste
To: Kim, Natalie
Sent: September 26

I just got back from the MD's office.

He did the ultrasound today because I am a psychotic freak. I told him about my dream about Jamie's baby and about me thinking this baby has ambiguous genitalia. He is so nice and understanding. He said that it is very difficult to diagnose ambiguous genitalia on ultrasound because you can see external genitalia but nothing internal ... so you don't know if there are ovaries or undescended testes or what going on internally.

He didn't say that he looked at the sex of the baby, but he told me not to worry. The heart looks great and he can't see anything that would indicate the heart problem that my friend's baby had.

Here is the kicker:

He said right now, at thirty-six weeks, the baby is between 7 pounds 9 oz and 7 pounds 11oz. How accurate is that?? (I didn't ask.) I am thinking the planned c-section is a good idea at this point. Especially if this baby gains the estimated "half pound per week in the last month" that they all talk about.

He checked me and said that I am closed and unless I start having contractions, they are only going to check the heart rate, blood pressure, and measure the belly until I go in to deliver.

I told John and he said, "Wow, so if you went to term with this baby, then it could be well over 9 pounds!"

I said, "Yes. Do you now understand why I am so uncomfortable? This baby is the same size right now that Anna was when I delivered her." He said he understood ... but they (men) will never truly understand.

From: Kim
To: Celeste, Natalie
Sent: September 26

I am glad that he checked out all those things and your baby is fine and normal. I think that if they do an ultrasound they are pretty accurate on the weight ... otherwise it is just a guess.

I had my MD visit today and have had absolutely no change. So we discussed my plan of action. I will have my membranes stripped a week from today to see if that moves things along, although statistically it only does something for 1 in 7 women so I really don't see the point in having it done. If that doesn't move things along, I will unwillingly schedule an induction for October 5th.

Can you tell how incredibly irritated I am getting? The prediction on my baby's weight about three weeks ago was lower 7's but I have gained quite a bit of weight since then and am now guessing she will be in the 8's somewhere.

From: Natalie
To: Celeste, Kim
Sent: September 26

I think they are pretty accurate on the weights as well. My doctor said 7 pounds for me if I went to my due date and he was 7 pounds 0.9 oz. I'm glad your babies are cooking up to perfection.

Kim, pray to Saint Gerard. He is the patron saint of expectant mothers. I prayed to him on Wednesday, July 26th and went into labor two days later. I prayed for a safe delivery and happy baby. I didn't want to get too specific with him since he was probably busy. I was willing to try anything. I will say a prayer for you too.

Celeste, what are we praying for you? Do you want to go into labor early so you can have an early c-section and not a 9-pound baby or what? The thing is, I pray more now than I have in a long time. I pray for all my pregnant friends and of course for Gager. I figure he just came from heaven so he has a direct line of sorts to the big man.

I went back to the MD today to check the southern hemisphere of Guentherland. She used the silver nitrate again to burn the tear. She said my body has over healed on the inside (which will inevitably cause bleeding with intercourse—oh joy) and not healed enough on the outside. She cleared me for all activities (sex, horseback riding, etc.) and said if I have excessive bleeding or pain in three months come back. I think I'll tell Brad I need to wait another year. Think he'll buy it??

COME ON, SAINT GERARD! He's busy but he'll answer you ASAP!

Dr. Bob says

Postdates or post term is defined as greater than 42 0/7 weeks gestation. The incidence of post term/postdates has been reported to be as high as 3 to 12 percent. However, it is most likely significantly less frequent and continues to become less frequent and may be a thing of the past.

Now, with our ability for more accurate dating criteria and the better recognition of both mom and baby risks increasing with post term/postdates, we can better predict a due date. There is at least a twofold increase in stillbirth compared to term. There are also increased risks for growth restriction and other adverse outcomes for babies delivered post term compared to term.

The risks to mom are also increased including abnormal labor curves, increased c-section rates, increased risks for perineal tears or lacerations, bleeding and infection. How long to let a pregnancy go remains unanswered. However, most current date and recommendation would suggest somewhere around forty-one weeks.

From: Kim
To: Celeste, Natalie
Sent: September 27

My due date was yesterday. I am on the brink of tears every minute. I have been asked four times already why I am still here and I have been at work for forty-five minutes. I would not mind going over so much if I could just stay at home and be in my own mental zone, but I have to deal with everyone else. We got five phone calls last night too. Here I am, trying to do the right thing and let her come on her time and not mine, but everyone else keeps harassing me about it, including my parents! I am so frustrated. I think I will cut them (my parents) out of my will. Can't everyone just leave me alone?

Delivering the Truth

Have you ever really sat down and done the math on how long you are pregnant? We did and although we are social workers, we do know that forty divided by four equals ten. So there you have it, "It's Really Ten Months."

From: Celeste
To: Kim, Natalie
Sent: September 27

Yea. I think it is a good idea to cut your parents out of your will and put me in their place!

I might get to the point where I don't read any emails or answer the phone.

It would be nice if we had enough leave from work to take a week or two off before the event happened, that way there would be no, "You are STILL here?" comments from the peanut gallery. I am continually being asked when I am taking leave. Um, I am having a baby on Oct 12th, so I will be taking leave from Oct 12th until whenever.

And they all say, "What? You are working the week of the 12th? You are working on the 10th and 11th?" Umm ... yes. If I had ten years of vacation, then maybe I would take a day to get my nails done, but no such luck, so I will be here.

Anyway, bottom line, Kim: you are doing the right thing in letting the baby come when she is ready and writing your parents out of your will. Both are very reasonable and understandable.

From: Kim
To: Celeste, Natalie
Sent: September 27

Are you frickin' kidding me? You have a scheduled date of when your child is going to arrive and they keep asking you? I think you should put major laxatives in their coffee anytime one of them asks. (Did you ever see *Dumb and Dumber*? I hate to admit that I did but the idea of someone being miserable with the runs because they asked a stupid question gives me great pleasure right now!)

From: Natalie
To: Celeste, Kim
Sent: September 27

Cutting your family out of your life when you are about to go into labor is quite reasonable.

People are jerks. Remember in biblical times where the pregnant women were separated from everyone except other pregnant women and were not allowed to come home until they got their periods again. They had the right idea.

I second the motion that you are doing the right and brave thing by waiting. I am a firm believer in avoiding an induction if you can. I too was ready to schedule the induction at the end when I swore I wouldn't. You just get so freaking sick of being pregnant. But this is all part of the little trick God plays on you in order to get you ready for labor. It's happening, Kim. You are doing great.

And, Celeste, I had those dumb ass people ask me if I was going to work up until I delivered. Well let's see ... the hospital doesn't give maternity leave so damn skippy I'll be here until ... well ... until my water breaks in the office and I drive home to shave my legs.

October 12th. I will be up to see you on October 13th after a phone call to make sure you are accepting visitors and you are finished with your psych consult.

From: Kim
To: Celeste, Natalie
Sent: September 27

Now see ... this is the shit I need ... voices of reason. Thank you. My sanity is somewhat restored (until tomorrow when I have an all-staff meeting and have to listen to a whole new set of people who convey their shock that I am "still here").

From: Celeste
To: Kim, Natalie
Sent: September 28

I tried *The Sleep Fairy* and Anna wasn't that interested. She tried it for a while and then she didn't want to read the book anymore and didn't care about the gifts left under her pillow.

So now it takes her over an hour to go to bed because she is constantly up out of bed, trying to get out of her room, crying, screaming, throwing a fit, you name it. It takes all the restraint I have not to haul off and smack her on the butt. I have not done it, but I am surprised I have not.

I am going to buy the *Super Nanny* book today and see what she has to say about it. Do either of you have any ideas? I asked Jennifer this morning and she didn't. I see the pediatrician on Monday to recheck her ears and I will ask him too.

Honestly, how am I supposed to put her to bed for nap or bedtime when I have a baby? It doesn't help that I have a short fuse and need her to nap and go to bed so I can get things done that I can't do with her awake.

From: Natalie
To: Celeste, Kim
Sent: September 28

I am of no help in the toddler sleeping department. I hope your MD will have some good advice. Do you think she's misbehaving because of the baby, or just being naughty?

How cool that your friend Jennifer is going to come and help after the baby is born! Honestly, having my sister here to help was a life saver.

Oh crap. Crying kid. More later.

From: Kim
To: Celeste, Natalie
Sent: September 28

I have been thinking about this for a few hours now. I always think back to what the child behavior specialist at work says, so don't take offense to this! The first question that would be asked is, "What is your reaction to her?" She is getting something out of it even if it is your negative response.

I am betting you have already done this but this is all I can really think of. When she gets out of bed, don't talk to her. Take her by the hand and lead her back to bed. Do not give her any positive or negative reinforcement by responding to her. Drag her back to bed kicking and screaming if you must but don't respond to her other than a simple, "Good night."

On *Super Nanny*, she has the parents do this even if it is 500 times in a row. The next night it ends up being about 400 times and so on. Let her open the door and come out because you (and John if he is home) can take turns politely taking her straight back to her room and into bed.

I love watching the *Super Nanny* even though it is the same damn lesson for parents over and over. Please save this email and send it back to me when my daughter is two. I would appreciate it very much, especially if it works.

 From: Natalie
To: Celeste, Kim
Sent: September 28

That is true about *Super Nanny* and that is what she explains in her book. I bought the book when I was still pregnant because I refuse to have bratty kids. (We'll see how that works out for me.) Can you give her Nyquil? Just kidding. Sort of.

Two-month shots for Gage tomorrow. I get to hear that ear piercing cry that makes me freak out into full on mother mode. I'm so looking forward to it.

 From: Natalie
To: Celeste, Kim
Sent: September 29

Gage got his shots today. That terrible scream came out. It actually made me tear up. So this is motherhood ... wow!

October

From: Natalie
To: Celeste
Sent: October 2

Any word on Kim? I don't dare ask her for fear of the overdue pregnant woman's wrath.

From: Kim
To: Celeste, Natalie
Sent: October 2

I just realized our kids (mine and Celeste's) are going to be about a week apart in age. I don't know if I should laugh or cry since we were supposed to be a month apart.

Interestingly enough, people are starting to say today, "You're still here? I bet you are getting tired of hearing that, huh?" Umm yes, I was tired of hearing it last week too if you really want to know.

One gal said, "I bet you hope you don't have to have a c-section, huh?" Yes, you are correct. I was hoping to have a vaginal delivery but why the hell bring that up only to add another worry?

Then another said, "I had my membranes stripped and it was horrible. I had the worst cramps for a few days. Then, since it didn't work, I had to be induced. You are going to have an epidural, aren't you? That will help with how bad the contractions are ... " What the hell? Are these really stories I want to hear on a Monday morning before 9:30?

And finally, I have grown out of this bra too. I know we didn't think it would be possible but I do believe I am probably an F now as my DD is bowing out at the sides and rubbing my arms. I simply refuse to buy a new bra until I start lactating. I really do not understand people wanting a boob job. These girls are so grotesque in my opinion. I have already told Ben that after we are done having kids, I will be getting a lift and fix 'em job to get back to how they were before my trauma.

There's a spider in my window. I hate spiders.

 From: Natalie
To: Celeste, Kim
Sent: October 2

Well, at least you two will have your maternity leave together. That will be great. You can be unshowered crazy women with kids hanging off of your boobs together—and that is priceless.

Kim, my heart goes out to you. You are handling this very well. The fact that you haven't killed any of the stupid people is quite noble.

I will refrain from commenting on the size F boobs until I am assured you will not kill me and get off the hook by claiming pregnancy hormone imbalance.

You both realize that once you are done popping out those kids that we have to get together for dinner.

Brad said he'd pay for a personal trainer for me once his baseball season is over (so he'll be home and I can actually go to the gym). I brought it up—he's not being a jerk here—he just knows I'm not pleased with the state of my body. At this point I don't care if I have to be at the gym at 5 a.m.—these rolls have got to go!

From: Kim
To: Natalie, Celeste
Sent: October 2

That's cool he is agreeable to that! I can already relate to how you feel. I find my body absolutely disgusting right now and there is still a baby in there. Ben and I were sitting in the hot tub last night and I was stating this and he most sincerely said that he thought it was the most beautiful thing in the world. I still don't believe him.

From: Celeste
To: Natalie, Kim
Sent: October 2

Brad and John are on the same page. John completely understands my body image issues right now and says he is willing to do anything to help me with this, which in theory is great, but he forgets that he travels. And what happens with the kids when he is traveling?

Kim, you need to give us an update after your doctor's appointment. Is it today or tomorrow, I can't remember.

I got the baby room put together yesterday—crib made, mobile up, everything cleaned/washed so I guess I am as ready as I will ever be. We also bought a new monitor, new diaper pail, and two-person stroller (thanks to Kim's coupons).

I am thinking I should put up the Halloween decorations this week or that will never happen. But I am afraid if I put them up, they won't come down until December when I put up the Christmas crap. Oh well.

From: Kim
To: Celeste, Natalie
Sent: October 2

I laid a horrible guilt trip on Ben but I don't think he knows that's what I was doing. I told him that I had researched the whole "stripping membranes" thing and how his sperm would basically do the same thing and how painful it would be to stick a finger through something that was only as big as 1 cm and blah, blah, blah. So girls ... I might actually see some action for real tonight. Not that it sounds fun by any means and I really don't want him touching me but better him than the doctor! God would he be so humiliated if he knew I was telling you this. Ha! Too bad!

I am game for dinner. Hell, if I have to return to school right away, I am sure I can handle going out to dinner! I put up our Halloween decorations yesterday. Now that I am having an October baby instead of September baby, I intend to fully brainwash her into loving Halloween as much as I do. And as far as your decorations go, all the stores have their Christmas items up before Halloween so what does it matter that you will have your Halloween items up when Christmas rolls around?

I'm glad the coupons worked for you. They had some pretty good deals in there!

From: Kim
To: Natalie, Celeste
Sent: October 4

Well, isn't this a pleasant experience. I woke up every hour last night with contractions. Of course, they only last 30 to 45 seconds so there is no point in going up to the hospital just to have them send me home. And losing my mucous plug was like having a banana slug in my underwear. And having these contractions that radiate to my back every three to five minutes is also fun.

But the best part is the fact that she seems to have moved off my one nerve and onto my sciatic nerve. All of a sudden I will have back pain that shoots down my leg(s) and I have to hang onto something so I don't fall over. I swear to you, ladies ... if this child does not come today I will go crazy.

From: Natalie
To: Kim, Celeste
Sent: October 4

Yahoo! Sneezing in the shorts and pain in the back are great signs!

It's happening. Hang in there (then again ... where would you go?).

Shit. Crying kid ... fun, fun!

From: Kim
To: Natalie, Celeste
Sent: October 4

So, I'm not sure, but I think I might be having contractions. The nurse from the hospital just called to do my pre-admit for my induction on Sunday and I told her what was happening. She said I should just come in. I called Ben and we are going to head up around noon.

Celeste, I will call and let you know if I actually am in labor and when I get close so you can take pictures. I really don't think this will be it.

 From: Celeste
To: Natalie
Sent: October 4

I just talked to Ben. Kim is in labor and is staying, but from what I gathered, things are not progressing well ... I'll let you know more if/when I hear anything.

 From: Natalie
To: Celeste
Sent: October 5

Have you heard anything? What is the deal?!

From: Celeste
To: Natalie
Sent: October 5

She just called. She labored FOREVER and ended up with a c-section ... poor woman. I will call you with her name and stuff and we can decide when we can go to visit!

From: Kim
To: Natalie, Celeste
Sent: October 8

Thanks for visiting me guys. Gage is getting so BIG! With all the visitors, I didn't have a chance to share the details of what happened and I really think I need to process ... so here goes.

I was sitting here thinking about this and realized that I was scheduled to have an induction today—October 8th, which would have put me at twelve days past due. As you remember, I did not want to be induced because I knew my chances of needing a c-section would go up. I also did not want pitocin or stadol. Besides ... why not let my body do what it is supposed to do naturally anyway right?

Well, at my MD appointment on October 3rd we finally decided that if this baby wasn't coming on her own I would need to be induced. Neither my doctor nor I were comfortable going over two weeks. When you have a scheduled induction, a nurse contacts you to do your admit stuff so the nurse in Labor and Delivery doesn't have to do all of it.

Wednesday morning I am having mild contractions. My abdomen is tightening enough to be slightly uncomfortable but not pull out your hair and scream pain. The admit nurse happens to call so we do my pre-admit stuff. Then I tell her what is going on and that what is concerning is that I am having the "contractions" about every two minutes but they are only forty-five seconds long. She tells me I might want to go ahead and just come in since I am overdue anyway and probably in labor. I call Ben to come home so we can go up to the hospital around noon.

We get there and I disrobe for the nurse to check me. I am still only dilated to one! What!?! Is this a sick joke? So they have me walk around for an hour to see what happens. Mind you, we all know that Wednesdays can be busy days for inductions. Apparently everyone who was going to deliver at my hospital in October came in the same day I did. It was busy.

We didn't really have one particular nurse assigned to us yet. This didn't bother me in the least because I knew that I would get taken care of regardless. We walked around for an hour and there was absolutely no change. I was then told I could go home or go ahead and be induced. This was the dilemma. We had intended to get induced the following day but because the schedule was full the entire week we had to wait until Sunday. So if we decided to get induced today, then it was really only one day sooner than we had intended but four days sooner than we were actually scheduled.

We decided to stay. I knew I would not sleep or rest with the contractions the way they were regardless if they were painful or not. I think it was around five o'clock that they decided to go ahead and break my water to see if that would get my contractions going.

No such luck. Have I said at this point how extremely uncomfortable it is to have your cervix checked multiple times without an epidural? Now the contractions are hurting because there is no fluid around the baby to cushion the blows. What was worse ... there was meconium in the water. I really tried not to freak out and think I may have done an okay job.

Since my cervix refused to dilate, they decided to start the pitocin. Remember that I did not want to have pitocin? Sweet God in heaven above—my worst nightmares are true. The contractions were excruciating! It seemed like they came every minute although I was informed they were coming every two minutes (big freakin' difference if you ask me!).

I could not breathe. I attempted to crawl out of the bed away from the pain but I could not. Ben told me he had no idea that I had that kind of strength in my hands and how he wished he would have taken his ring off first because I was squeezing his hand so tight.

The nurse told me that I wouldn't be getting an epidural until I was at least 3 to 4 cm because they didn't want it to slow things down. I cried. Yes, I cried in front of a complete stranger and felt like a weak, weak woman. She checked me ... I was at 2 cm. I didn't think I could take it. I finally relented to the stadol. I was told that it makes you loopy and most people don't like it. I am here to tell you that it took the edge off my pain enough so I could breathe. Thank you, God, for stadol. Thank you.

Sadly, it doesn't last too long so an hour later I think I am near death (or praying for it) again. One of the nurses I used to work with came in to say hi. She took one look at me and told the other nurse that I should probably go ahead and get an epidural. Praise Jesus. I about started crying right then and there. Ooooh yahh ... I had already been crying. She is definitely going in my will.

I asked how long it would take for the doctor to come up (I know the hospital isn't big but it can take ten minutes to walk from outpatient surgery to L&D, which is a lifetime at that point). Before I even finished the sentence, the anesthesiologist god came running in. I am not kidding ... he ran. Remind me to write him into my will too.

Now, people have told me that the epidural is nothing compared to contractions ... and they are totally correct. However, my contractions hurt so bad I didn't think I would be able to stay still for him. I always thought I would and could when the time came but let me tell you, when that next contraction came on, it was a good thing he was almost done.

I asked how long the epidural would need to take effect. He said, "One to two more contractions." Too long in my book but oh what a relief when it started to work. I actually could start breathing again.

Once it was on board my thought was, "Shoot, with this working I could deliver ten babies because I can't feel a thing!" I had wanted my favorite anesthesiologist to give me the epidural but he wasn't on until later in the night and, quite frankly, at this point, I didn't care if the mailman gave it to me as long as someone did!

Later in the evening I still wasn't dilating. My doctor came and worked on my cervix a bit. There was some scar tissue. I think the verdict is still out if that is why I wasn't dilating. Nurses think yes, doctor thinks no. I don't care at this point.

I slowly start to dilate. The baby starts to decel after the contractions. This is when working on the OB unit in a previous life does you no good. You can tell when they are watching the monitor with that certain look on their face that it is not good. Then they come in to place an internal monitor. This is more good news. They have me lie on my left side. They have me lie on my back. They have me stand on my head (okay, now I am being dramatic).

I don't think Ben realized what "decelling" really meant but I knew that if things didn't turn around quick I was having a c-section. We all knew I did not want that! Meanwhile, the anesthesiologist I did want to do my epidural comes in and chats with us for a while. It was nice because both the doctors were hanging out and chit chatting. On the other hand, they may have been staying close by which again made me think things weren't going smoothly.

She starting doing better after a little while but that didn't last too long. After she picked back up she then started a new trick ... she became nonreactive. I got on my hands and knees to see if that would help. It did not. The doctor probed her head a bit ... that didn't help. My doctor was well aware that I did not want a c-section.

She looked at me around midnight and said, "I don't think we can wait any longer, I'm sorry." Fortunately, there wasn't a question in my mind about seeing if I could dilate two more cm so I could do a vaginal delivery. She obviously could not tolerate labor any more and I was fine with a c-section.

I cannot believe how quick they can get you ready for a c-section. It seemed like she had said that and I was in the surgery room in the crucifix position. The doctor assisting had been the one who broke my water earlier in the day. My doctor was standing on a stool (she apparently wasn't tall enough!).

I was shaking so bad from the medication that my chest muscles hurt and all I could think about was how I wanted this over so I wouldn't hurt so bad from shaking. I am pretty sure that the assisting doctor was trying to push all of my internal organs up and out through my mouth while my doctor was trying to get the baby out. I hated every minute of the procedure. It was sterile and my body ached from reacting to the anesthesia.

Suddenly, I felt immense relief and she was out! I kept listening for her to cry and she didn't, which made me so nervous. Had I been thinking clearly I would have realized that there was a team there to work on getting everything suctioned out of her mouth so she didn't swallow any of the meconium that was in the water. How can one think clearly in such barbaric situations? (Can you tell that I am now, more than ever, not an advocate for elective c-sections?)

She finally cried and Ben brought her over to me. Honestly, girls, I felt such a disconnect. You tell me this is my baby but I didn't watch her come out of me ... all I saw was a blue drape in front of me while all the doctors talked about what was on *Grey's Anatomy.*

Then I see a reflection in the huge light above me with something like a red balloon on my stomach. Silly me actually asked what it was at which point the assisting doc said, "That would be your uterus ... you want that back on the inside." I asked if they could do a little liposuction while they had me open but apparently this was not an option.

They took me to recovery where I was blissfully able to sleep for two hours. So much for delivering my daughter and having skin-to-skin contact within minutes of delivering, then breastfeeding within twenty minutes. So much for a peaceful moment of getting to know this little person that I carried around for nine months (let's cut the crap, for me it was 10.5 months). When they finally brought me down to the room, they brought her down for only a few minutes because she wasn't breathing well enough and wanted to watch her.

So I finally, after nine hours, was able to have her in the room and feed her. And then there was visitor after visitor. Who knew I could function on so little sleep? She was the most perfect little baby! I could not believe that she was as beautiful as she was. I think that is really the only benefit of my c-section experience was that she wasn't all mashed up from a regular delivery.

I only stayed in the hospital for three days. I do regret that ... next time, if I have the misfortune of having another c-section, I will stay all four. Getting out of bed to feed her without the magical hospital bed that moves up and down is way too painful. I seriously think I am ripping out internal stitches. Is this possible? I will have to ask my doctor.

So all in all ... after she was finally in my room, things went well. I never put her in the nursery because I slept just as well with her in the room and didn't want to worry about what she was doing in the nursery. I will keep you posted on how the first few days go. Thank God Ben has a week off work to help!

Meet Giselle Marie

Born October 5, 12:19 a.m.

Weight: 7 pounds 15 ounces

Length: 21 inches long

Dr. Bob says

Let me address more delivery issues: Contraction intensity increases after the bag of water breaks? Why? There is no consensus here. It goes across the board. Some report increased intensity with contractions after the bag of water breaks, others do not. It may have more to do with where in the labor process you are rather than the fact the bag of water breaks, or is broken.

Meconium-stained fluid is when the baby has a bowel movement in utero and excretes meconium, which is a thick green-black tarlike substance that lines the baby's intestines during gestation. Meconium-stained fluid occurs relatively frequently, between 10 and 15 percent of pregnancies.

Meconium-stained fluid in and of itself does not mean your baby has or is having any problems. However, it does result in closer observation because occasionally it can be associated with other evidence that may indicate the baby is not enjoying the intrauterine environment. Meconium aspiration syndrome occurs when the baby not only swallows the meconium, but gets it into its lungs. This is very uncommon, only about 5 percent of those pregnancies have meconium-stained fluid. So only in about one half of 1 percent. If it occurs, it can be a serious condition.

How fast can a c-section occur in emergencies? It depends on where you are and the situation surrounding the need for cesarean section. Although certain time constraints have been put forth, it is felt that it should be done as expeditiously as possible. In level III hospitals, it will generally be able to be done quicker than in small community hospitals, but there is no absolute.

Ripping internal stitches. It's normal to have the sensation that "everything is going to fall out of my incision" after a c-section. It won't. Although in very rare situations it is possible for the internal (fascial) sutures to come loose or break.

Decels (decelerations) is a term used in reference to the fetal heart tones. To adequately discuss these is way beyond the scope or intent here. It suffices to say that they are changes in the baby's heart rate that occur in labor. They are early, variable, late, and prolonged decelerations. Although decels can be associated with concerns in labor, more often than not, decels are not associated with any adverse outcome for baby.

From: Celeste
To: Natalie, Kim
Sent: October 8

Wow, that was a long night for you! I am really sorry you felt like there was a disconnect between you and Giselle because of the c-section. But you are correct, c-section babies do come out looking so pretty! And she is a doll, by the way. It was great visiting you. Now that you are home, we need to get you through the hormonal stage and then my delivery, and then we can all get together again!

From: Natalie
To: Celeste, Kim
Sent: October 8

I agree, Kim. You kind of got kicked in the shorts with the whole laboring and then topping it off with a c-section. Bottom line: she's here, and she is SO CUTE. It was great seeing you! You looked like a natural sitting in your rocking chair holding your daughter.

Okay, Celeste, you're on deck ... LET'S GET READY TO RUMBLE ...

From: Celeste
To: Kim, Natalie
Sent: October 9

On that note I feel like I have a cluster of grapes coming out of my ass. Is that too much information?

From: Kim
To: Natalie, Celeste
Sent: October 9

If you were talking to the general public, then yes. Since it is us ... no.

From: Natalie
To: Kim, Celeste
Sent: October 9

I think we've surpassed the TMI barrier, don't you think? We've all shared too much now. Bundle of grapes? Nice visual. At least you won't have to push a kid out through the bundle of grapes.

Hey, Kim! How's it going?

Celeste, I hope you are having a boy because I got you kind of a boyish present—but it comes with a gift receipt. ☺

From: Kim
To: Celeste, Natalie
Sent: October 9

Update on life with a newborn.

Last night went fairly well. My milk came in the night before and was in full force yesterday. I was dripping as I walked around the house. I was majorly engorged last night, which was quite painful. My nipples are cracking a bit, and I know that means she is not latching on right but all other signs indicate a good latch on so who knows WTH is going on.

Anyway ... I had to pump a little last night before my boobs exploded. This turned out to be a good thing because I dumped it in a bottle for Ben to feed her at 3:00 a.m. I slept from nine to midnight and then she woke up. She then cluster fed until 3:00 when I decided the bottle wouldn't crack open and bleed one more time like my boobs would.

She then slept until 5 a.m., I think, and woke a little so I brought her to bed so I could feed her but she fell asleep. We did too (sleep that is) and none of us woke up until about 8 a.m. So we did the co-sleeping thing. Oops. I don't care. She is a really good baby and I am feeling quite optimistic.

My engorged boobs are slowly deflating but I have decided I am going to pump a little after each feeding (which the books say I can do). She took to the bottle right away and I was standing right there.

She is too cute. She will wake up and stare at you like, "I know you are someone or something that I should know, but right now I am going to examine you as if you are an alien life form."

I hate c-sections. I do feel like I was totally robbed of my birthing experience. I have a friend who says c-sections are the only way to go. Since when is slicing your body open the only way to go? I can barely move around, which makes the whole breastfeeding thing a bit difficult.

I can say I am pleased at how quickly my body is reducing in size (well, my tummy anyway ... my ass and hips are still quite large and we don't need to talk about my boobs). By the way, Ben said, "You know your boobs are big when I can see them from behind." ☺ He has been totally awesome.

I will keep you posted. I believe I am five days away from the emotional breakdown so you may see my emails decline from this point on.

From: Natalie
To: Kim, Celeste
Sent: October 9

Well, it sounds like the breast feeding is going well. As Celeste said, if you can do it for one day that is better than nothing. I've been telling everyone how cute she is but I don't have any more pictures to back it up. She has such grown-up features.

I'm glad that Ben is being great. He seems to have the fatherhood thing down, which should keep the stupid comments to a minimum. As far as c-sections—WTH? Three out of four of us (including Jamie) get c-sections. Do I have no one to bitch with about the sore nether regions? You guys will be in your skinny jeans and having romantic nights with your husbands in a week. I'm not bitter.

I always enjoyed the ole air drying of the boobs or as my doctor said, "Walking around like Madonna with the flaps down." I did this when I was alone ... no need to scare anyone.

I have a problem with my pants. My pants fit. They go on and zip but they squeeze a huge roll above the waistline. It's terrible. Shirts don't cover it up it just looks disgusting. The gym daycare doesn't take babies until they are six months.

I nearly killed Brad when he said he's going to drop Gage off at the daycare we are going to use for two hours every day while he goes to the gym. Isn't the whole point of him staying home so we cannot expose Gage to daycare in the winter? IF ANYONE IN THIS HOUSE GETS TO GO TO THE GYM IT SHOULD BE ME!!

Is that too much to ask?

Take care! Email when you have time (hahahahahahahaha!).

 From: Kim
To: Natalie, Celeste
Sent: October 10

I thought I had sent you pictures! I will send a few when I have time.

I agree. You are the one who gets to go to the gym. This is non-negotiable. I wish I could mourn with you about the nether region pain but even if I had a vaginal delivery ... would anyone really be able to relate to you? You kind of win that race, hands down.

Lactation consultants called me today. Despite my raw nipples they seem to think I am doing well and this is normal. She predicted by Thursday or Friday that I wouldn't feel raw anymore. I do need to work on a deeper latch on though. All in good time.

Meanwhile, Ben will run to Target today to grab some slow flow nipples. I hope they work since she is having a harder time with the bottle. ☹ I walk around with the flaps down. Ben laughs and says how funny it looks. I don't care. It feels good. So do the Soothies ... best things invented ever!

From: Celeste
To: Natalie, Kim
Sent: October 10

I just want to say that it sucks being the last one pregnant. I knew this would happen ... but it sucks nonetheless.

Not that I am excited to be in the breastfeeding, no sleep, kid attached to me 24/7 mode, but honestly ... DONE WITH PREGNANCY!

Glad to hear that Ben and Giselle are both being good at their jobs. If Giselle continues her current sleeping pattern, I am going to be more than jealous. And if I don't get as much milk as you, I am going to be jealous. I am telling you, pumping and having anyone else but me feed breast milk is a great idea and one that I hope will work for me too ...

Have fun with that emotional breakdown phase ... always a highlight.

Brad is going to the gym and you are not? What is wrong with him? Doesn't he see how crappy you feel about your body?? Doesn't he understand you will not be a normal human until you can wear all the same clothes you had prepregnancy and look better in them than when you were two weeks pregnant? Boys.

I was in this same predicament when I had Anna ... and now I have the treadmill. The only way I got the treadmill was telling John that if he really loved me, he would buy me the treadmill for Mother's Day.

So might I suggest investing in workout videos and/or a treadmill. This is honestly the only way you will get to work out before Gage can go to the daycare at the gym, which isn't that great. I only took Anna there twice because the girls in there were very hands off and didn't play with the kids.

From: Kim
To: Celeste, Natalie
Sent: October 10

I hope this kid wakes up soon. She always decides she wants to eat when someone brings food over. This is my life for the next eighteen years ...

Last night she cried and cried and cried until midnight. Slept until 3 a.m. I fed her. Slept until 5 a.m. I fed her. Woke up at six and Ben brought her to bed with him where she slept until 8 a.m. He took her out and worked on the bottle feeding thing and I slept until 9 a.m. I don't look forward to when he returns to work.

From: Kim
To: Celeste, Natalie
Sent: October 10

I forgot two things ...

First, my first BM was not horrible. Not wonderful but was certainly better than the significant one that I wrote a ten-page email on before and far better than Natalie's. This is worth celebration in my book.

Second, although I have seen *Independence Day* a thousand times it made me bawl today. I was holding Giselle and I noticed that I was feeling very anxious when the world was being blown up and thinking what I would do and where I would go with her if that happened. This mom thing sure makes you vulnerable.

On another note, Ben went out and bought a new nipple for our bottle (before I realized we already had the right size). It worked beautifully! I am definitely in favor with the gods. I hope this continues to work. No one told me not to laugh after a c-section. Dear Lord, the pain is unbearable.

Five more days to go until my breakdown.

Delivering the Truth

Now you are completely responsible for protecting another human being. Is there any more pressure than that?

From: Celeste
To: Kim, Natalie
Sent: October 11

Kim, I distinctly remember telling you that I made sure I took all my drugs and had a pillow to hold over my belly while watching *American Idol* (the auditions) after my c-section with Anna. You must have been in a new mom haze when we had that discussion, but you can't say I didn't try to warn you!

I am glad your first BM wasn't horrible. They will continue to get better.

Do I need to tell you again how jealous I am that the gods are being nice to you? I just know they will hate me and punish me for all the horrible things I think and sometimes say out loud. Who knew this is how karma worked?

May I remind you that tomorrow is my last day as a mother of one. I don't know if I'll have a chance to email again before I go to the hospital since Jennifer and John's mom are both coming in town. I guess there are some benefits to having a scheduled c-section. I'm bringing my laptop so we can send an email with pictures to all of our friends. If I feel up to it, I'll email you guys after delivery.

From: Natalie
To: Celeste, Kim
Sent: October 11

Girls, girls, girls ... let me remind you that you will both be blessed with speedy recoveries. All the bad crap was dished out to me because God has a very weird sense of humor.

Celeste, enjoy your last day of freedom. I'll call you tomorrow afternoon to hear your son's name (oh yea, I have decided it is a boy) and make sure you are doing okay and then I'll come see you on Friday—if you are drugged enough to be up for it. My mom is coming today so I think I'll hand off the kidlet and loaf around town. YAHOO!

Kim, sounds like things are great ... lucky girl.

Damn. Screaming kid. Later taters.

 From: Kim
To: Celeste, Natalie
Sent: October 11

Good luck, Celeste! I'll be anxious to hear if it's a boy or girl.

 From: Natalie
To: Celeste, Kim
Sent: October 11

So last night and today I've been on the phone with the Boys Town Pediatric Nurse on call or whatever it is to figure out if we need to start Gage on soy formula. He's been extra fussy for the past few days. After he eats, when I put him over my shoulder to burp him, he's been screaming bloody murder. Yesterday he had this lovely green mucus in his diaper, and his bottom is all red and he has a bit of a rash on his cheeks and chin.

According to my handy dandy book this means a food allergy. The nurse on the phone gave me a very lovely answer of, "Try soy if you want to." WELL LADY I DON'T WANT TO TRY

IT! I DON'T WANT TO PAY 80 ZILLION MORE DOLLARS FOR FORMULA IF I DON'T HAVE TO.

Now I have a call into my doctor to see what she says. I'm down to like three more bottles worth of formula before I have to crack open a new can, and I don't want to open it if he can't use it. I hope it's not an allergy. I'm sure she'll say buy a can of soy and see how he does. The only helpful info I got last night was that they want you to try a new formula for two to three weeks before trying something else. I guess he's right on schedule for a change.

Today he's less fussy and no green mucus, but he still has the rosy cheeks and chin. WTH??

From: Kim
To: Celeste, Natalie
Sent: October 11

I think that the nurse should be shot for being so unhelpful to you and the Gagemeister. Like you want to sit there and watch your child in discomfort while you "try" a new formula.

Poor Giselle almost sucked off the scab on my boob today. I felt horrible and it looked nasty. She took the bottle again last night for Ben. I'm hoping this good trend continues and someone isn't playing a horrible trick on me. I keep waiting for the other shoe to drop. She sleeps for three to four hours at a time. Sometimes more and then I have to wake her. I keep thinking she will wake up when she is hungry, but all the books say not to let them sleep past five hours (which, I admit, she has done).

On another note, there is nothing on TV to watch during the day except all the baby stuff. I found I couldn't watch the ones where they have a vaginal delivery because it brings tears to my eyes. I told Ben that I truly hope that my next one is delivered that way because I really feel like I have missed out on that bonding experience. I'm glad they did a c-section though so she is okay.

 From: Celeste
To: Kim, Natalie
Sent: October 13

Well ladies, what can I say? I guess I will start with getting checked in ...

This was better than last time because I actually went in knowing what time I was going to have the c-section and that I was actually going to have a c-section! Anyway, I get checked in at the crack of dawn ... by the night nurse ... who was fresh out of nursing school, but was really friendly. She starts my IV and stuff, and then she is going to give me a catheter (yuck!) so she has the crew (John, my mom, his mom, and Jennifer) leave. But you know what that means if she is going to give me a catheter ... yes, she has to look at the veins.

So, I have to warn her. I tell her:

Celeste: "I must warn you, I have issues down there."

Naïve little nurse: "Oh, you have hemorrhoids?"

Celeste: "Oh yes, I have those too. But along with the cluster of grapes coming out of my ass, I also have varicose veins where no woman should have varicose veins."

Naïve little nurse: "Oh! I have heard about that and read about it in my nursing books, but never seen that!"

Nice ...

Moving on ... the crew comes back and then within about thirty minutes my doc arrives and we get the ball rolling! This time I got a spinal in the OR instead of an epidural ... I liked the spinal better. And I was hell bent to stay lucid during the delivery and not get all freaky and need drugs like last time.

I was fine, a bit claustrophobic, but not bad enough to get extra meds to knock me out. He cuts me open and pulls out little Robert. John, of course, was thrilled to have a boy! He went out and told the crew. Then once the nurses got him all cleaned up, they wrapped him up and let me hold him until they sewed me back up. He was 8 pounds and 19 ½ inches long ... and ten days early ... imagine if I would have gone full term!

Anyway, the first thing I noticed about him—he looks EXACTLY like John—and he might have red hair, the jury is still out on that one!

Anyway, everything went great—100x's better than my c-section with Anna. No pain control issues and I'm out of bed today and got to take a shower. I am a new woman after that shower! Can't wait to see you guys. Come visit whenever it works out best for you. I am not going anywhere.

Meet Robert Leonard

Born: October 12th, 8:16 a.m.

Weight: 8 lbs 0.6 oz

Length: 19 ½ inches long

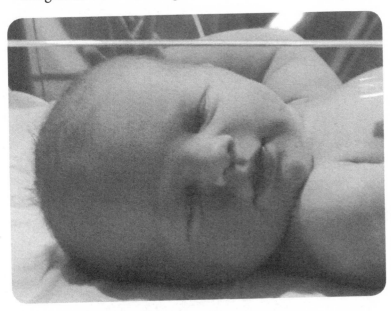

Epilogue

SIX MONTHS LATER ...

From: Natalie
To: Kim, Celeste
Sent: March 9

I might be crazy but ... I think we should write a book. Seriously. About all the stuff we went through during (and after) our pregnancies. We can't be the only women in the world who experienced elephantiasis of the boobs or created crop circles ... What do you guys think?

From: Celeste
To: Kim, Natalie
Sent: March 9

Really? I think that would be pretty cool. Ya know, I have all of our emails. Only because I am lazy and never delete anything from my Inbox.

From: Natalie
To: Kim, Celeste
Sent: March 9

What! You didn't delete those? Who does that? Anyway ... wouldn't it have been nice to have a book like that? Maybe then we wouldn't have been so naïve.

From: Kim
To: Natalie, Celeste
Sent: March 9

Ummm ... Celeste, how many emails do you have in your Inbox?

A book! Some of those emails were really funny ... like the ones about maintaining the nether regions. Oh, and did you save the horrible one about Nat's bathroom experience? I will forever be in debt to the makers of Colace.

But I think you guys should know, I am not going to have a lot of time to work on a book because ...

I'M PREGNANT!

Glossary of Terms

Braxton Hicks—fake contractions, you know, to get you ready for the real thing

BRU—Babies R Us

Colace—the magical pill that helps you poop

CPS—Child Protective Services

Decelerated (decel)—when the heart rate monitor shows baby's heart rate drops and everyone (unnecessarily) freaks out

DINKY—Dual Income No Kids—Yet

Glucola—that orange syrupy delicious-ness you drink to check for diabetes

Hoyer Lift—a contraption where you put your butt in a sling and it lifts you up

Kegel exercises—twat-squeezing exercises

Mastitis—bad boobie infection

Meconium—the baby's first poop, which resembles sticky black tar

NICU—Neonatal Intensive Care Unit

Perinatologist—a fancy pregnancy specialist (and if you are lucky, you get Dr. Bob)

PITA— Pain In The Ass

PPD—post-partum depression

Pylo—kidney infection

Quad screen—optional blood test done around sixteen weeks

TMI—Too Much Information!

UTI—urinary tract infection

WTH—What the Hell! And, of course, WTF—what you say when WTH isn't quite strong enough

Meet the Authors

Natalie Guenther

The creative writer and dreamer. This is the poor soul who thought she'd be lunching with friends and leisurely shopping while on maternity leave. Poor thing didn't even see the truck that hit her. Natalie holds a master's degree in social work and works in the field of brain and spinal cord injury rehabilitation. She, her husband, and their three kids live in Omaha.

Kim Schenkelberg

Although sarcasm is often her tone, she counts on her friends to know that underneath it is a caring soul. A sojourner at heart, she remains firmly planted in Omaha, the city of her birth until she is free again to travel. Kim obtained her master's degree in social work soon after she delivered her first child. She practices in the fields of domestic adoption and therapy. She is married to a man who could win husband-of-the-year awards nearly every year because of his big heart. Kim is a stepparent to two quickly growing boys. She has two daughters and one son with her husband. Lord help them. This is one crazy busy clan of seven!

Celeste Snodgrass

The first four letters of the word analytical are what—yep—anal. This type A leader of the pack is the one who saved months' worth of emails for this project. Celeste has earned her master's degree in social work. She currently works in the field of international adoption (this feeds her need for intense organization). Celeste, her hilarious husband, and their two children live in Omaha.

Connect with us!

Facebook.com/ItsReally10Months
Twitter.com/Really10Months
Instagram.com/ItsReally10Months
Pinterest.com/Really10Months
ItsReally10Months.com
ItsReally10Months.com/blog

If you liked this book, you'll love our second!

Makes a great shower gift!

It's Really 10 Months Special Delivery:
A collection of stories from girth to birth
ISBN: 978-0-9888668-4-3
Price: $15.95

Purchase the book at ItsReally10Months.com or Amazon.com
Available on Kindle and other e-reader formats